Nuclear Policies:
Fuel Without the Bomb

Nuclear Policies:
Fuel Without
the Bomb

Albert Wohlstetter
Victor Gilinsky
Robert Gillette
Roberta Wohlstetter

With a Foreword by Robert F. Bacher

A POLICY STUDY OF THE CALIFORNIA SEMINAR ON
ARMS CONTROL AND FOREIGN POLICY

Ballinger Publishing Company ● Cambridge, Mass.
A Subsidiary of Harper & Row, Publishers, Inc.

CALIFORNIA SEMINAR ON ARMS CONTROL
AND FOREIGN POLICY

The Seminar, founded in 1970, has an active program of research, discussion, and publication on the issues faced by governments in foreign policy and arms control. It is jointly sponsored by the California Institute of Technology and the Rand Corporation. Funding for the preparation of this book came largely from the Ford Foundation.

The Seminar welcomes and encourages diversity in the viewpoints and backgrounds of contributors. It does not take an institutional position on the issues it considers. The views expressed in this book are those of the authors.

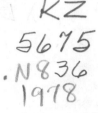
 This book is printed on recycled paper.

International Standard Book Number: 0-88410-084-7

Library of Congress Catalog Card Number: 78-13724

Printed in the United States of America

Library of Congress Cataloging in Publication Data

Main entry under title:

Nuclear policies: fuel without the bomb.

    At head of title: California Seminar on Arms Control and Foreign Policy.
    1. Nuclear nonproliferation—Congresses. 2. Atomic power—International control—Congresses.
I. Wohlstetter, Albert II. California Seminar on Arms Control and Foreign Policy.

JX1974.73.N8   327'.174   78-13724
ISBN 0-88410-084-7

Contents

Introductory notes for the chapters were written by James Digby, who organized the book and selected or commissioned the essays.

Foreword

Perhaps the most serious consequence of the worldwide dissemination of nuclear materials and technology over the past twenty years is the mounting number of nations that possess or soon could possess nuclear weapons. The oil embargo of 1973 strongly enforced latent desires for energy independence, turning many nations, industrial and nonindustrial alike, toward nuclear energy as a means to that end. The press toward nuclear power and independence has led to actions and policy plans that will greatly increase the number of nations with quick access to highly enriched fissile material—the most vital ingredient of nuclear weapons—as part of their power programs.

The essays assembled in this book have, for the most part, grown out of studies of the nonproliferation of nuclear weapons conducted by the California Seminar on Arms Control and Foreign Policy during the past three years. The essays address technical, political, and economic aspects of nonproliferation in language that can be understood by specialists in all three fields. The Seminar held a major conference on prospects for nuclear proliferation in May 1975 and subsequently issued a series of eight derivative publications. This was followed by a round of meetings, principally organized by Albert Wohlstetter, presenting the views of officials of the U.S. government, of European experts, of the International Atomic Energy Agency (IAEA), and of specialists from the nuclear and power industries. Discussions of this kind, increasingly effective in the past year or two, have been followed by the passage and signature into law by President Carter of the Nuclear Nonproliferation Act of 1978. Nuclear proliferation is clearly a global problem, and the debate continues, both in the United States and abroad.

Growth in energy use has been rapid since World War II, especially in the developed nations. This growth has been accompanied by a decrease in the use of coal and a major increase in the use of oil and gas. The rise in energy use and the shift to oil and gas were due principally to the low prices for oil and gas and the convenience of their use. The development of nuclear power after World War II was greatly slowed by competition with oil at two dollars a barrel, a cost so low as to invite wasteful practices in energy use. The per-capita energy consumption in the United States is roughly twice that in Western Europe, where until recently most of the oil and gas has been imported. Many buildings in the United States were designed with inefficient heating and cooling systems because it was cheaper to waste energy than to provide for more efficient energy use.

It has been clear for some time that the rate of increase in energy use in most of the developed world, if continued undiminished, will inevitably lead to serious economic and political difficulties. Oil reserves, although very large, cannot last indefinitely. In the United States, until recently the world's largest oil producer, demand has exceeded supply for many years; we now import almost as much as we produce. The oil embargo of 1973 brought this situation strongly to the fore, although even then there were some who doubted the existence of a long-range energy problem. The fivefold increase in oil price, therefore, has been a real strain on oil-importing nations. At the same time there have been large increases in the cost of coal and gas, with more increases likely in the future. A major effort is now being made to conserve energy, and, of course, every nation is striving for energy self-sufficiency. In spite of conservation efforts, the United States will probably import more oil in 1985 than it does today. Although new industrial plants can be designed for more efficient energy use, many years of capital expenditures will be needed to achieve the desired results. Meanwhile, the amount of energy saved is likely to be relatively modest, except in the areas of transportation and space heating.

It probably will not be possible to solve our energy problems by conservation alone. In 1974–1975, total energy consumption in the United States decreased, but this was accompanied by a decrease in gross national product (GNP). The extent to which energy use and GNP are tied together is debatable; but it is unlikely that GNP can be increased year after year without a rise in energy consumption, even in the United States, where energy waste is greatest.

The need for new energy sources had led to many proposals and much research and development work. Major sources likely to provide an increasing amount of energy in the future are coal, nuclear fission, solar radiation, and nuclear fusion. Other possibilities for significant new energy production include the tapping of geothermal heat and, farther in the future, the use of indirect solar energy (e.g., thermal gradients in the ocean), the tides, the wind, and even the biomass. Some of these sources, such as geothermal energy, are available now to a limited extent. In many localities, the use of solar energy for space and hot-water heating is also feasible, although it may not be economically competitive even against present high fuel costs. Even though such sources as fusion or solar electricity show promise for the future, they still present many problems, and the likelihood of significant commercial use in the next generation is small.

Thus, the principal energy sources until somewhat beyond the end of this century seem to be coal, oil, gas, falling water, and nuclear fission—with supplementation from other sources in minor amounts. Furthermore, in spite of sporadic discoveries of new supplies of oil and gas locally in many areas, the major reserves lie in the Middle East. New hydroelectric sources, especially in the developed countries, have limited possibilities for expansion. Therefore, it seems inevitable that we will turn increasingly to coal and nuclear energy, the former being unlikely to meet the major U.S. energy needs alone. Coal production, after falling for many years, is only now back to its 1920 level. In addition, there are serious pollution problems; all new coal-generating stations in the United States in the future must be equipped with means for removing sulfur dioxide (SO_2) from the stack gases. Furthermore, the burning of any fossil fuel in large quantities presents a long-range problem: the production of carbon dioxide (CO_2) to the extent that its fraction among the atmospheric gases is increased, raising the temperature of the atmosphere by the so-called greenhouse effect. The CO_2 content of the atmosphere is unquestionably increasing, but the whole process of release and dispersal is not fully understood. In sum, there is probably trouble ahead if we continue to draw energy principally from the combustion of fossil fuels. This means that long-range energy sources will probably be solar, nuclear fission, or nuclear fusion.

For all these reasons it is likely that for the next generation we in the United States will be using more nuclear fission energy. What is likely in this country seems almost certain in Western Europe, Japan, and some of the less developed countries. Japan has almost no energy resources, and those of Western Europe are much less copious than they are in the United States. There will be strong national forces for achieving energy independence.

The construction rate for nuclear installations will nevertheless be considerably smaller than that predicted five to ten years ago, chiefly because of the slower growth of energy demand. Also, the enormous capital demands for new electricity-generating stations has caused many electric utility companies to postpone new plant construction. Indeed, all new generating stations cost much more than they did a decade ago; and even though the capital cost for a nuclear generating station is somewhat more than that for a coal plant of the same size, the cost difference is no larger than the range of costs between coal plants in different locations. Operating costs of nuclear plants are generally believed by utility company managers in the United States to be somewhat lower than those of coal plants. Costs worldwide are not easy to determine, but it would be surprising if they differed radically from U.S. figures in developed countries, even though environmental requirements elsewhere may be less stringent. In short, cost in developed countries will not be the deciding factor between coal and nuclear fission energy. Perceived advantages for greater national independence will be important, and it is likely that nuclear energy—with as much independence or ensured continuity of fuel supply as possible—will be preferred.

These are the principal reasons why Japan, Canada, West Germany, Britain, France, Spain, Brazil, Taiwan, South Africa, and other countries have moved toward nuclear energy. They are likewise the reasons why many nations have pressed for facilities to reprocess spent fuel elements and to separate the contained plutonium (Pu) produced in light-water reactors (LWR) so that it can be used for fuel. As fuel for LWRs, this Pu would be sufficient to give only a little more independence and little, if any, saving in cost.

In less developed countries, costs of nuclear power facilities will probably be greater both to install and to operate than in developed countries. There may be wide variations in cost from one country to another because of their need for special engineers and technicians and large capital investments. Countries, such as OPEC members, with excess oil supplies will not gain any additional energy independence. They may even become more dependent on others for their nuclear fuel.

Many developed countries, and possibly some others too, have plans for building breeder reactors that actually produce more fissionable material than they burn. From the viewpoint of fuel supply in the long-range future, such a procedure is attractive. From the viewpoint of the proliferation of large amounts of plutonium, it is dangerous. With the present likely, but not proved, uranium reserves, the nuclear power program can probably be fueled for the next thirty years without breeder reactors. After that, breeders or some other major source of energy besides coal will probably be needed. This is indeed a risky prediction, depending both on the estimated demand for central station power and on the available uranium supplies.

It was this situation that prompted Presidents Ford and Carter to postpone the construction of reprocessing plants that would produce Pu from the spent fuel rods of nuclear power reactors, and to urge other nations to do likewise. It was also this situation that prompted President Carter in 1977 to withdraw his support for the Clinch River Breeder Reactor. This demonstration breeder reactor has not progressed as well as had been expected, and it is present U.S. policy to look into alternative breeder possibilities that do not necessarily involve separated Pu.

The possession of highly enriched fissile material—U–235, U–233, or Pu—is, of course, a critical factor in producing nuclear weapons. The reader unfamiliar with these technologies can gain an idea of their relevance in the chapter written by Robert Gillette. Highly enriched U–235 has never been widely available, although Britain, France, and the Soviet Union have had it, and the Soviets apparently transmitted information (and perhaps materials) for its production to China. Until recently U–235 separation required a very large gaseous diffusion plant to produce fissile material adequately enriched to make nuclear weapons. The next plant to be constructed in the United States to produce slightly enriched U–235 for reactor use will employ the centrifuge method. Such a plant built to produce 3 percent U–235 for light-water reactors can probably be reconnected without major reconstruction to produce weapons-grade U–235. Furthermore, laser and possibly other separation methods lend themselves to the direct production of highly enriched U–235 capable of being used in weapons. Uranium highly enriched with U–235 will be much more easily available in the future unless steps are taken to monitor and control its spread. The production of U–233 from thorium is carried out in a reactor, producing highly enriched fissionable material; but this product could be denatured and made unfit for weapons by diluting it with U–238. Although reactor-grade Pu from power reactors is not ideal for making nuclear weapons, it is quite adequate; this fact has been known for a long time. Albert Wohlstetter covers this point in depth.

The general concept of producing an implosion nuclear weapon is now sufficiently widespread, and the needed arts are now sufficiently advanced that any nation with moderate technical capabilities should be able to produce a nuclear device, whether the fissile material is highly enriched U–235 or Pu of either weapons or reactor grade. With reactor-grade Pu the yields from different weapons might vary somewhat, but real fizzles would not be expected. A delivery system is essential to the effective employment of a nuclear weapon, and sophisticated delivery vehicles are not simple to produce. However, a sophisticated delivery vehicle is not absolutely required; indeed, some delivery vehicles may be developed or purchased openly as part of a nonnuclear weapon system procurement program. Fissile material, then, is the vital ingredient today in the production of nuclear weapons. The exploration of this subject and what should be done to limit or slow the spread of nuclear weapons is the principal subject of these essays.

Views differ as to the degree of monitoring and control of fissionable material required for adequate security against the spread of nuclear weapons. The IAEA was set up to monitor the fissionable material used in reactors for peaceful purposes. This monitoring, however, does not cover all reactors worldwide. Indeed, it is doubtful whether monitoring alone can provide meaningful security against weapons proliferation where stocks of highly enriched material are widespread. Of those nations that have produced nuclear weapons since World War II, essentially all those in the Western world have moved first to produce plutonium; later they have produced nuclear weapons either openly or secretly. If weapons development were accomplished by a nation secretly, very few weeks would be needed to produce nuclear weapons once highly enriched fissile material were available.

The pressure for a nation to join the "nuclear weapons club" is very strong, if as part of its long-range energy program it has augmented nuclear reactors with its own reprocessing facilities and if it has, or expects to have, a sizeable stock of highly enriched fissionable material. The ease of the move makes the achievement of big-power status difficult to renounce from a narrowly nationalistic point of view. As more nations join the nuclear club, other nations with nuclear power programs but without stocks of highly enriched fissile material may find it increasingly difficult not to tag along.

In the spring of 1977 President Carter declared that the United States would forgo the reprocessing of spent fuel elements and the separation of the contained Pu until a solution to these problems could be found. He proposed storing spent fuel elements in the meantime, a procedure that has been used successfully for a decade or more. He urged other nations to do likewise and not to export reprocessing plants, which in some cases had already been contracted for. As might be expected, this proposal met with vigorous opposition from those expecting to build such facilities as well as from the exporting nations. The proposal was also attacked by the nuclear industry generally. The situation is still unsettled. Clearly, no solution can be achieved by the United States unilaterally or by pressuring other nations to do as we propose. This has recently been made clear by Britain's decision to go ahead, after much controversy, with the large Windscale reprocessing plant. In addition, West Germany has concluded a contract with France for the reprocessing of large amounts of spent fuel elements, an action that will probably lead to the construction of additional reprocessing facilities in France. All these facilities will probably produce Pu, and the accumulated stocks will soon be large and widely dispersed. By an ironical twist, most of this Pu was produced in light water reactors with slightly enriched fuel that came from the United States as a part of the Atoms for Peace program.

Nevertheless, the realization is growing that the world is on the verge of an irreversible step toward much more widespread possession of nuclear weapons. This concern is shown by Australia and Canada, which—along with the United States and South Africa—are probably the principal sources of natural uranium in the Western world. Both countries will probably put restrictions on the end use of the uranium they export. The passage of the U.S. Nuclear Nonproliferation Act of 1978 provides limits on export policy to ensure that nuclear materials, equipment, and technology exported for peaceful uses will not be diverted to produce nuclear explosives. This act also encourages the production and export of nuclear reactor fuel "to nonnuclear weapon states only if such states accept IAEA safeguards on all their peaceful nuclear activities, do not manufacture or otherwise acquire any nuclear explosive device, do not establish any new enrichment or reprocessing facilities under their de facto or de jure control, and place any such existing facilities under effective international auspices and inspection." If a moratorium on proliferation can be achieved, a lasting and effective international solution may still be possible.

Victor Gilinsky suggests in his essay that it might be possible to internationalize reprocessing control. This point goes back to the farseeing Acheson-Lillienthal Report of 1946, which became the pattern of the proposals made that year by Bernard Baruch on behalf of the United States in the U.N. Atomic Energy Commission. The essence of this proposal was that it separated "dangerous" nuclear activities and put them under the control of an international Atomic Development Authority. The Soviet Union rejected the proposal, which would have included all weapons activities and the enrichment of fissile material. It is interesting that, thirty-two years later, we have returned to the point where some activities must be considered dangerous and where a halt to the spread of nuclear weapons can be achieved only by serious international control of these activities.

In his second essay Gilinsky expands on the idea of international control, discussing how much control is necessary to be effective for highly enriched material. Because of the short interval between the acquisition of highly enriched materials and their possible incorporation into nuclear weapons, controls are required that do more than merely sound a warning. This higher level of control can be achieved only by more extensive international limitations than are imposed on the operation of nuclear power plants. The limitations, for example, must cover the fuel cycle as well.

It has often been said that the easiest way for a nation to acquire nuclear weapons is to follow the path that India took. Roberta Wohlstetter recounts the sorry story of how India built and exploded a nuclear device (purportedly a peaceful nuclear device, whatever that is) with significant help from the United States and Canada. This help was given so ambiguously and with such sloppy controls that there is room for doubt whether the Indians even violated the letter of the restraints, even though the spirit of the restraints was clear enough. For a nation without a nuclear power program, the Indian pattern could be followed. A research reactor would serve for producing Pu; but the production would be very limited, and it is likely that large research reactors will arouse more suspicions in the future. These suspicions would come long before any nuclear weapon could actually be prepared; but, as in the case of Israel or South Africa, it is doubtful whether anything would or could be done about it internationally. This is not the path, of course, for developing a nuclear capability of significant size.

The Indian example shows what can be done with relatively modest facilities and a covert program. Consider, then, the potential threat offered by a nation faced with a mortal crisis and possessing a sizable nuclear power program in which spent fuel is reprocessed, Pu separated, and a sizable stock openly accumulated for the needed continuity of reactor operation. If the nonnuclear weapon components had been developed covertly, a nuclear complement could be brought together very quickly. In this sudden act of proliferation lies the greatest threat: a real—not an imagined—danger for the future.

The proposals of Presidents Ford and Carter met with the expected opposition. There are nevertheless some signs that nations engaged in selling nuclear reactors and reprocessing equipment are beginning to realize the critical and irreversible nature of their trade. It may just be possible, although it is not really likely, that this critical situation can be turned around, making the future less ominous rather than more so. This cannot come about by unilateral U.S. action, but only by some form of international agreement.

Robert F. Bacher

Pasedena, California
April 1978

Nuclear Policies:
Fuel Without the Bomb

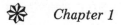 *Chapter 1*

Nuclear Technology: Essential Elements for Decisionmakers

Robert Gillette

Policies influencing the spread of the technologies by which nuclear bombs might be made are clearly among the most important being formed by lawmakers, government officials, and citizens. Yet the technical complexity of the underlying factors serves to prevent much of the wisdom of people concerned with these policies from being applied in a consistent and informed way. In this chapter Robert Gillette explains the technology of nuclear energy production and relates this to bomb-making in a style that is comprehensible to the nonengineer, and that serves as background to the remainder of the book.

Nuclear proliferation can advance by a variety of routes, some of which the international community has worked harder to obstruct than others. The most direct and obvious ways in which nations or subnational groups might try to obtain nuclear weapons are to steal, buy, or borrow them. Although the successful theft, purchase, or loan (or gift) of weapons is not inconceivable, it can at least be said that a number of important political and technological obstacles have been strewn along this route. These range from generally high levels of physical protection for weapons to built-in disabling devices to the Nonproliferation Treaty of 1970, under which parties agree not to help others in any way to obtain atomic weapons.

NUCLEAR REACTORS AND NUCLEAR WEAPONS

Barriers to weapons are significantly fewer along a very different route, one that has become the locus of renewed concern about proliferation in the 1970s: the sale of civilian nuclear power technology. The connection between electric power reactors and weapons is an unfortunate consequence of nature. For the same three fuels that reactors can burn to make electricity—plutonium and two isotopes, or closely related forms, of uranium (U-235 and U-233)—are also the only substances that are practical to use in fission weapons.[a]

Thus the proliferation problem, as it has come to be perceived in the past few years, centers on this dilemma: How can the world-wide demand for peaceful nuclear power best be satisfied without inadvertently endowing dozens of additional countries with latent stockpiles of nuclear weapons?

Happenstance and the laws of physics relieve this dilemma in some respects and complicate it in others—and inevitably influence the kinds of barriers that might be built between commercial nuclear power and nuclear weapons. For instance, the two easily fissionable forms of uranium (U-235 and U-233) can be diluted and rendered impractical for use in an explosive—some authorities prefer the term _denatured_—by mixing them with U-238, the most abundant form of uranium. The two types of power reactors in widest use today burn uranium fuel that is too highly diluted with U-238 to make a bomb. And separating weapons-grade uranium from this mixture is almost universally considered a difficult technical feat, although it may not always be so.

But this barrier to weapons is offset, and the proliferation problem greatly complicated, by the fact that highly diluted uranium generates large amounts of plutonium as an unavoidable by-product of nuclear fission. Plutonium can be separated from spent reactor fuel by chemical processes that are simpler than the refinement of weapons-grade uranium. Moreover, plutonium, unlike uranium, cannot be diluted and denatured by other isotopes; all forms of this heavy metallic element can be used to make an explosive, although the necessary amount is greater for the heavier isotopes.

Thus, any nation that stockpiles purified plutonium for use as a civilian reactor fuel has, in principle, the option of converting it to weapons in the face of a real or imagined threat—quickly, if it has troubled to build the nonnuclear parts of weapons in advance.

Alternative nuclear power and fuel systems have been proposed that would reduce or avoid the production of plutonium, or would make it less readily accessible for conversion to weapons. The practicality of these ideas, however, is still very much open to conjecture, and even their most ardent proponents acknowledge that technological fixes alone are unlikely to suffice.

---

[a]The spread of thermonuclear fusion weapons is not at issue. Fusion weapons release energy when the nuclei of lightweight substances, such as lithium and the two "heavy" forms of hydrogen (deuterium and tritium), are heated to tens of millions of degrees centigrade under enormous pressure, and fuse. A sophisticated fission explosive is required to trigger this reaction in a fusion weapon.

The linkage between peaceful and military applications of nuclear energy has, of course, been a source of international concern since the advent of fission technology in the 1940s. But two recent and unrelated developments have helped drive proliferation issues to new prominence on the American foreign policy agenda. These are the rapid rise of world oil prices in the early 1970s and India's detonation of a nuclear explosive in May 1974.

Among developing and industrialized nations alike, the oil price rise and the Arab embargo of 1973 greatly intensified interest in nuclear energy as a means of reducing the consumption of costly and politically vulnerable imported oil. To avoid simply shifting dependence to imported uranium, many nations envisioned extracting by-product plutonium from spent reactor fuel, purifying it, stockpiling it, and eventually recycling it in power reactors.

From these plans arises the prospect that, by the mid-1980s, more than thirty countries will potentially have the plutonium on hand with which to build nuclear weapons.[1]

Broad new interest in proliferation was prompted by the rise of international terrorism in the late 1960s. Initially, public and government attention centered on the problem of physically protecting nuclear fuels on the chance, however remote, that subnational groups or even a small, independent band of sophisticated terrorists might steal enough to fashion a simple but effective bomb.

The Indian test of May 1974 brought a gradual but important shift in the focus of this burgeoning discussion. Although the physical security of nuclear materials has remained an important issue, U.S. government—if not public—attention has swung toward the behavior of governments themselves. The Indian test suggested not only that many countries were capable of building nuclear explosives but also that peaceful power and research technology could provide a crucial stepping stone to weapons. In constructing its explosive, India, after all, had used plutonium produced and stockpiled ostensibly as part of a civilian research program aimed ultimately at building plutonium breeder reactors for electric power.

Four years later, it is now widely accepted that most governments could, as a contingency measure, design, build, and test the nonnuclear components of weapons with at least a moderate chance of maintaining secrecy and without violating international nuclear safeguard agreements. In a national emergency, civilian stockpiles of plutonium (or weapons-grade uranium, if it is available) could be diverted to complete a small but significant arsenal in a short time, in days or conceivably hours, leaving the international community little time in which to detect, much less react to, this potentially catastrophic step.

Spokesmen for the U.S. nuclear industry acknowledge that this scenario is technically feasible; nevertheless, they regard it as improbable.[2] It has, in any case, formed the driving paradigm of new nonproliferation policies in both the Ford and the Carter administrations which have culminated in fundamental changes in American energy supply strategy. Most important, if only as gestures of earnestness, are the decisions of the Carter administration to defer indefinitely the recycling of plutonium as a supplement for uranium fuel and to postpone commercial development of commercial breeder reactors.

The Carter objective has been to buy time to examine global institutional changes and technical adjustments in nuclear fuel systems that might alleviate the proliferation problem as it is now perceived. To the extent that technology can help, the solutions it provides will be governed by crucial similarities—and differences—in the physical properties of the three nuclear fuels.

NUCLEAR REACTOR TECHNOLOGY

The most important shared feature of plutonium, U-233, and U-235 is that their atoms readily split, or undergo fission, when struck by neutrons.[b] When an atom of plutonium or uranium fissions, it breaks into two smaller, highly energetic atomic nuclei called *fission fragments*; these in turn emit two to four more neutrons, then decay radioactively to form the dozens of different isotopes that constitute the waste products of nuclear fission.

If enough fissionable fuel is arranged in the proper shape, or geometry, to interact with itself, the result is a chain reaction of splitting atoms and rapidly multiplying neutrons. (The minimum, or threshold, amount needed to start a chain reaction is called a *critical mass*.) Most of the heat from a chain reaction comes from the collision of flying fission fragments with surrounding materials; but large amounts of energy are also liberated in the form of gamma rays and beta particles.

In a reactor, the chain reaction is kept under control mainly by moving neutron-absorbing control rods into a core of fissioning fuel. These manipulations allow the removal of all but a small surplus

---

[b]The numbers refer to the sum of the neutrons and protons in the nucleus of an atom. The positively charged protons (and a matching number of negatively charged electrons orbiting the nucleus) determine an atom's major chemical properties and thus its identity as one of the known chemical elements. Neutrons have almost the same mass as protons but carry no electric charge. Their number affects the mass and nuclear stability of the atom, but, except for the lightest elements like hydrogen, has little bearing on chemical properties. For practical purposes, isotopes of heavy elements are chemically identical.

of neutrons needed to sustain the chain reaction at the desired power level.[c]

In a bomb, by contrast, the chain reaction is deliberately uncontrolled. A chemical explosive compresses the uranium or plutonium into a supercritical mass momentarily (less than a millionth of a second) but long enough to trigger a violent fissioning of at least a few percent of the fuel. The complete burning of one kilogram (2.2 pounds) of uranium or plutonium yields about the same energy as the explosion of 17,000 tons (17 kilotons) of TNT, roughly the power of the weapons that destroyed Hiroshima and Nagasaki.

The amounts of the three fissionable fuels commonly accepted as sufficient to make an explosive—which, as a consequence of physics, is most likely to yield 1 to 20 kilotons with simple designs—can be carried in one hand: 5 kilograms (11 pounds) of plutonium or U-233, and 15 kilograms (33 pounds) of U-235.[d]

Although all three materials are roughly equal in their explosive potential, kilogram for kilogram, the proliferation debate since 1974 has focused largely on plutonium. This emphasis reflects a broad consensus that weapons-grade uranium, for technical reasons, is more difficult for potential diverters to obtain and will remain so for some time.

By any measure, isolating U-235 in a purity adequate for use in weapons currently entails formidable technical challenges, even for highly industrialized nations.[e] Although for practical purposes it is the only naturally occurring substance that can sustain a fission chain reaction, U-235 makes up only 0.7 percent of uranium as it is mined. The rest, except for traces of other isotopes, consists of U-238, which undergoes fission only when bombarded with very high-energy neutrons. (Some of these are released in the fission process, but they are not abundant enough to sustain a chain reaction in U-238, thus preventing its use as fuel for a reactor or a bomb.)

---

[c]High-energy neutrons produced in a fission reaction are not as easily captured by uranium or by the material in a control rod as are less energetic neutrons. Therefore in order to improve neutron capture and thus enhance the fission chain reaction it is desirable to introduce material into the reactor that "moderates" or slows down the fission neutrons to an energy level where they more readily interact with the uranium. The moderator needs to have atomic nuclei at nearly the same mass as a neutron as possible. Hence ordinary hydrogen is the most ideal atom, and water (H_2O) is a common form of moderator.

[d]Only small amounts of U-233, totaling about 1,000 kilograms, have been produced in the United States, chiefly for experimental purposes. It is not clear from unclassified sources whether it has actually been used in an explosive, although weapons authorities express no doubt whatever that it can be.

[e]New separation techniques are being developed, however, and isolating U-235 may not be so difficult if they prove to be practical.

To make a uranium explosive, the much more readily fissionable U-235 must be concentrated or "enriched" in an isotope separation or enrichment plant. In theory, a concentration of 7 to 10 percent U-235 is enough, although 20 percent is usually taken as the lowest practical enrichment level for a bomb; weapons designers prefer 90 percent or higher.

By contrast, the two most common types of power reactors in commercial use today—heavy-water reactors (HWRs) and light-water reactors (LWRs)—run on natural uranium fuel or uranium enriched with about 3 percent U-235 (see Appendix to this chapter). The U-238 that makes up the unburnable bulk of the fuel acts as a diluting agent and prevents its use in explosives.

Since the advent of nuclear weapons more than thirty years ago, the sheer difficulty and expense of enriching uranium—compounded by the heavy cloak of secrecy that the nuclear weapons states have, for the most part, maintained over enrichment processes—have foreclosed access to weapons-grade U-235 to all but a few nations.[f] The difficulty arises from the fact that U-235 and U-238 are two forms of the same chemical element and thus cannot be separated by ordinary chemical means. Instead, practical separation methods have relied on the small difference in weight of the two isotopes.

Even for those nations privy to the technology, enriching uranium is an expensive, cumbersome, and difficult business. The five nuclear powers—the United States, the Soviet Union, France, Great Britain, and China—currently use the gaseous diffusion process, in which gaseous (and high corrosive) uranium hexafluoride is pumped through porous barriers of materials such as sintered nickel powder or Teflon. The barriers preferentially pass the lighter U-235, but each barrier stage provides only a small increment of enrichment. Reaching the 3 percent level requires passage through about 1,000 successive stages; the 90 percent level preferred for weapons demands another 3,000 stages. In the United States, three gaseous diffusion plants (in Ohio, Kentucky, and Tennessee) cover hundred of acres, represent a capital investment of more than $10 billion, and at peak production consume about 6,000 megawatts of electric power, or 1.5 percent of the entire nation's generating capacity. Smaller gaseous diffusion plants can be built, but even the smallest practical size would be a costly and conspicuous enterprise.

A more energy-efficient and compact enrichment process using ultra-high-speed centrifuges is moving into commercial application in Western Europe and the United States; but the same mantle of

---

[f]A notable exception to this rule of secrecy was the Soviet Union's apparent provision of gaseous diffusion technology to China in the 1950s.

secrecy that helped restrict the spread of gaseous diffusion technology has held, so far, for centrifuge enrichment as well. Although a clandestine centrifuge facility is conceivable, its construction would require a high degree of technical sophistication, and perhaps a breach of or a deliberate change in a government's rules of secrecy.

Except for the nuclear weapons countries, only the Netherlands and West Germany, and to a lesser extent Japan, are known to be capable of centrifuge enrichment on a significant scale. A major uncertainty in the proliferation problem, however, is whether laser enrichment and other emerging techniques will greatly simplify the separation of uranium isotopes over the next ten to fifteen years, and thus lower the technological barriers to uranium weapons that have persisted now for more than thirty years.[g]

A different set of circumstances limits the global availability of U-233. Like plutonium, U-233 exists in nature in traces too minute to permit extraction from natural resources by any known means. It can be made in reactors by bombarding the radioactive metal thorium with neutrons, then chemically separating out the newly formed uranium. (In some ways it is a better weapons material than plutonium, for it is equally fissionable but far less toxic, an important consideration for people who work with weapons and who clean up accidents involving weapons.) Yet a government with reactors at its disposal would seem to have little incentive to make U-233 surreptitiously when it was already producing plutonium legitimately, indeed unavoidably, in the course of generating electric power.

Plutonium forms in the same general way as U-233. An atom of U-238, the unburnable bulk of commercial reactor fuel, absorbs a neutron. Instead of splitting, the atom becomes U-239; in a short time it undergoes two stages of radioactive decay, first transmuting into a new element (neptunium-239), then becoming fissionable plutonium-239.

This is the main form of plutonium, but another isotope, Pu-240, has figured importantly in the proliferation debate. This is a second-generation variety that forms when Pu-239, still inside the reactor core, absorbs a neutron instead of splitting. An unstable isotope, Pu-240 readily fissions by itself, emitting copious numbers of neutrons and complicating the using of plutonium in weapons.

---

[g]One way of obtaining large stocks of weapons-grade uranium without enrichment technology would be to buy a high-temperature gas reactor (HTGR). The commercial model offered by the General Atomic Company in the United States burns fuel enriched to 93 percent U-235. The largest HTGR in the United States is a 330 megawatt (electric) demonstration plant at Fort St. Vrain, Colorado. Although HTGRs offer several advantages over LWRs, such as greater thermal efficiency, General Atomic currently has no outstanding orders, and the worldwide future of the HTGR is uncertain.

At first it was widely believed that this isotope could be used (much like U-238) to dilute and denature the plutonium produced in power reactors, making it unsuitable for weapons. The reasoning was that the spontaneously emitted neutrons from Pu-240 would start a chain reaction prematurely, after the bomb's chemical explosive trigger had been detonated but before the plutonium core had reached the density, or state of supercriticality, essential to an efficient nuclear burn. The result, it was thought, would be a nuclear fizzle, or at best a weapon of highly uncertain yield.[h]

It is now known, however, that while the presence of Pu-240 may pose a problem for weapon designers, it can be overcome by relatively unsophisticated designs that will reliably yield between 1 and 20 kilotons. To emphasize this point, the U.S. government disclosed in September 1977 that the Los Alamos Scientific Laboratory had, in 1962, detonated a nuclear explosive in Nevada using plutonium typical of that produced in ordinary nuclear power plants.[i]

From the standpoint of proliferation, the most important difference between uranium and plutonium is that all forms of plutonium can be used in an explosive. Nothing can be added to make plutonium unusable for weapons—nothing, at least, that cannot be removed by chemical processing.

The amount of plutonium generated each year in a typical 1,000-megawatt power plant varies among reactor types. But the light-water reactors used in most countries produce about half a kilogram of plutonium for every kilogram of U-235 they burn.

Some of the fresh plutonium fissions while still in the reactor, adding to the power plant's heat output. Each year utilities replace about one-third of the fuel of a LWR; if the reactor has been running 80 percent of the time, the discharged portion will contain about 250 kilograms of plutonium, or the equivalent of thirty-five to forty nuclear weapons, each with a nominal yield of 20 kilotons.[3]

Put another way, a typical power reactor generates an amount of plutonium equivalent to one nuclear explosive every ten days.

This plutonium is not, of course, immediately accessible. It is too

---

[h]The proportion of Pu-240 in spent reactor fuel depends on how long the fuel has been in the reactor. Nuclear weapons countries minimize the design problems it causes by building special production reactors from which fuel is removed at an early stage of burn-up. In the United States military plutonium contains no more than 6 percent Pu-240, whereas that from civilian power reactors typically contains 24 percent. The Pu-240 content also adds to radioactivity, making the plutonium harder to handle, though probably not to the extent of deterring potential diverters.

[i]The design solution is one of speed. The faster a weapon's high-explosive detonator "assembles" the plutonium parts, the lower the probability that a stray neutron will start a premature chain reaction.

finely dispersed in the discharged or "spent" fuel to make an explosive. And the fuel itself, which consists of long, slender tubes of stainless steel or zirconium alloy filled with hard brown pellets of uranium oxide, becomes so intensely radioactive during its months in the reactor that direct human contact with it would quickly result in lethal radiation exposure.

The residual radiation comes from accumulated fission products trapped in the fuel. These include most of the same isotopes that make up the fallout from atmospheric nuclear tests; they also form the troublesome "high-level" wastes of nuclear power generation. Before the fresh plutonium and leftover uranium in spent fuel can be used—at least in power reactors as they are now designed and run—the fission products must be stripped away by chemical processing.[j]

It is at this juncture in the nuclear fuel cycle—the reprocessing of spent fuel—that the proliferation debate has come to focus.

THE REPROCESSING OF SPENT FUEL

Extracting plutonium from spent fuel, in spite of its intense radioactivity, is almost universally regarded as an easier task than enriching uranium to weapons grade. As India demonstrated, the necessary chemical processes are within the capabilities of even modestly industrialized developing nations (although India's nuclear establishment ranks high in the developing world). The nuclear weapons powers made the job easier by declassifying plutonium processing technology in the mid-1950s. Furthermore, the worldwide spread of expertise and design details has been furthered by French and West German companies that until recently marketed blueprints and hardware for fuel reprocessing plants.

The basic technology emerged from the U.S. Manhattan atomic bomb project in World War II. But the standard process in use today (called Purex, a contraction of "plutonium and uranium recovery by extraction") was developed in the United States in the early 1950s for weapon production and later adopted by private firms for commercial fuel reprocessing.

At the front or "head end" of a typical Purex plant, behind

---

[j]Spent fuel is spent only in the sense that entrained fission products degrade its performance by absorbing the neutrons needed to sustain the chain reaction. Upon removal, light-water reactor (LWR) fuel contains 0.8 percent U-235, or 0.1 percent more than natural uranium. Most of this surplus, which roughly equals the fuel value of newly formed plutonium, can be recovered in reprocessing. Spent natural-uranium fuel contains only about 0.3 percent U-235 and is not economically recoverable at present. Nor is reprocessing for plutonium alone generally considered attractive.

massive concrete walls that shield against radiation, a remotely controlled shearing machine chops the spent fuel rods into sausage-like bits and drops them into stainless steel baskets for delivery to a vat of hot nitric acid. The acid dissolves the uranium oxide fuel pellets and fission wastes but leaves intact the fragments of tubing, or cladding, that enclosed them; these contaminated hulls become part of the waste that must be sealed from the biosphere, although some proponents of reprocessing, arguing that reprocessing is necessary to reduce the volume of nuclear wastes, do not count them.

Once dissolved, the fuel slurry is treated with an organic solvent to separate the uranium and plutonium from the hundreds of fission products present. Then the uranium and plutonium are separated from each other and drawn off as liquid nitrates. They can also be converted to oxide powders for more convenient storage.

Plutonium oxide will make an effective bomb, although military production lines use it in metallic form. A number of countries have used plutonium oxide experimentally as a reactor fuel but it is not yet in commercial production. The nuclear industry in the United States and abroad envisions mixing the purified oxide with reclaimed uranium, bolstering it with additional low-enriched uranium, and fabricating a new "mixed oxide" fuel. One common criticism of this procedure is that no useful purpose is served by extracting purified plutonium from spent fuel, placing it only a short step from possible incorporation in weapons, only to recombine it with uranium at a fuel fabrication plant.

There is an appealing symmetry to the recycling of spent nuclear fuel, although some industry authorities acknowledge that its economics are marginal at best. Some governments, notably that of West Germany, view the recycling of plutonium in today's reactors as an important factor in reducing dependence on imported uranium. Others, like the government of Great Britain, which depends almost entirely on imported uranium for its nuclear power supply, believe that plutonium can be more efficiently used in breeder reactors of the future. The British nuclear industry is nevertheless seeking to build a $1.1 billion reprocessing plant for both domestic and foreign fuel at Windscale on the northwest Cumbrian coast, to be partly financed by Japan.[k]

---

[k]Nuclear industry representatives in the United States and elsewhere have long contended that plutonium recycling in LWRs would reduce overall uranium requirements by about 30 percent. This assumes, however, a stable population of reactors. The faster a nuclear power system grows, the smaller the benefit of recycling, as the greatest uranium demand comes from *initial* core loadings for reactors that cannot immediately contribute spent fuel for recycling.

IAEA projections indicate that recycling on a worldwide scale would have relatively little effect on the demand for uranium resources and enrichment

Above all, the global nuclear community views the early establishment of reprocessing and recycling as a vital precursor to the introduction of plutonium breeder reactors, the next major evolutionary step envisioned for fission technology. Without some form of reprocessing and plutonium reclamation, the breeder would be pointless.

The sticking point is that current plans would inevitably give rise to large and potentially vulnerable stockpiles of weapons-ready plutonium. Even if the plutonium were to be burned in existing light-water reactors, fuel fabrication facilities would need substantial working stocks. In West Germany, for example, a new depository built next to the ALKEM company's small mixed-oxide fabrication plant has a storge capacity of 5,000 kilograms of plutonium oxide.

THE PLUTONIUM SECURITY PROBLEM

On a worldwide scale, the quantities of plutonium potentially moving in civilian commerce by the mid-1980s are immense. In 1975 the IAEA estimated that by 1985 about 800 power reactors serviced by 17 reprocessing plants would have a cumulative plutonium inventory of 675,000 kilograms.[5]

This is probably an overestimate, as many countries, facing uncertain growth in demand for electric power, have since cut back their plans for nuclear capacity in the 1980s and 1990s. A more conservative estimate, counting only power reactors in operation, under construction, or firmly planned as of 1975—outside the five acknowledged nuclear powers—projects a world plutonium inventory by 1985 of 122,000 kilograms shared by thirty-one countries.[6]

Maintaining security over so large and fragmented an inventory of a substance as potentially destructive as plutonium is a challenge without precedent. The simplest and most direct solution is one proposed by the Carter administration: store spent fuel intact for an interim period of a decade or more and let its intrinsic radioactivity provide the main barrier to diversion. Other governments have resisted this solution, arguing that reprocessing is desirable economically and necessary as a waste management procedure. The Carter administration disagrees on both grounds. And an independent analysis of nuclear waste disposal sponsored by the American Physical Society concludes that long-term storage of spent LWR fuel is

capacity before the year 2000. In 1975 the IAEA projected a cumulative uranium demand of 3,830 thousand tons through the year 2000 (not including the Socialist bloc) *without* plutonium recycling, and 3,650 thousand tons with recycling. The difference of 180,000 tons is about equal to one year's uranium demand in 1990.[4]

no more difficult than disposal of concentrated fission wastes.

The solution to the plutonium security problem that seems to be favored by the nuclear industry in the United States and abroad is to consolidate fuel facilities—reprocessing, storage, and fuel fabrication—in a relatively small number of tightly guarded and closely inspected nuclear "parks." Clearly, if plutonium entered such parks in spent fuel and left only in new mixed-oxide fuel rods, this arrangement would reduce the risks of plutonium being diverted in shipment in a form readily convertible to weapons. A national government would still have the option, however, of diverting purified plutonium from stocks in its own nuclear park. Even if the park were to be operated under international auspices, the possibility of a national diversion remains, at least on the part of the government on whose territory the park was located. (Multinational fuel facilities would in any case not necessarily preclude national fuel facilities.)

It can be argued, and proponents of plutonium recycling do argue, that any reasonably sophisticated government seeking nuclear weapons can get them without dipping into its cache of "civilian" plutonium. It needs only to build a small natural-uranium reactor and a small reprocessing plant like India's. The drawback is that building an alternative plutonium supply system takes time. Most estimates center on a minimum of two to three years. Reactors and reprocessing plants are also conspicuous, if not by physical bulk and radioactive emissions, then by demands for special materials (such as ultra-pure reactor graphite or heavy water) or by virtue of talkative participants. Such facilities may also be hard to explain.

Whether or not a government pursuing this direct approach to weapons wanted to hide its intentions, a lead time of two to three years before plutonium was actually in hand would provide the international community ample time to detect and react to these activities. Australia is an interesting case. Scientists there already know how to build the weapon, being privy to nuclear secrets of the United Kingdom, but they do not have the necessary materials. By their estimates, it would take about two years to produce their first weapon.

If, on the other hand, secrecy were of paramount importance—as it might be to a signatory to the Nonproliferation Treaty interested in keeping its options open—a government would presumably want to shrink to a minimum the lead time between noticeable interest in weapons and actual possession. This it could do legitimately under the treaty by covertly designing and building the nonnuclear parts of weapons and holding them in readiness. Were this to be done, the IAEA considers that the elapsed time between diversion of "civilian" plutonium in purified form and completion of a weapon need be no longer than ten days. By contrast, the IAEA believes, starting with spent fuel (assuming some facility in which to reprocess it) would stretch this critical period to "weeks to months."[7]

This quick-diversion scenario, which many analysts find so worrisome, presumes that a nation would be willing to field untested nuclear weapons. History suggests that this is not unthinkable. Although the United States tested a plutonium bomb at Alamagordo before dropping one on Nagasaki, the bomb that had obliterated Hiroshima three days before was an untested uranium device. It is also worth noting that the Central Intelligence Agency believes that Israel has nuclear weapons but that it is unlikely to test them.[8]

THE SEARCH FOR SOLUTIONS

In October 1976, late in the Ford administration, the U.S. government began a concerted study of alternatives to the current concepts of Purex reprocessing and recycling of plutonium. One major objective of this effort, which continues in the Department of Energy, was to find ways of squeezing more energy from commercial reactor fuel while at the same time stretching the necessary lead-time between a possible diversion and the completion of a weapon. The longer the lead-time, it is hoped, the greater the chance that the IAEA's system of material accounting and inspection would sound a timely alarm.

A number of technical fixes—helpful, perhaps, if not sufficient in themselves—have been proposed and are likely to be reviewed by the forty-nation International Fuel Cycle Evaluation program convened in October 1977 at the behest of the Carter administration.

Several ideas would avoid reprocessing altogether. In the tandem fuel cycle, for example, spent fuel from LWRs would be burned a second time in natural uranium reactors. This is possible because the U-235 content of spent LWR fuel is significantly higher than that of natural uranium. Initial studies by the U.S. Arms Control and Disarmament Agency indicate that the tandem cycle could yield 30 percent more energy from the LWR fuel and, by burning U-235 down below natural levels, eliminate half the incentive for reprocessing.

One engineering difficulty is that the fuel rods used in most LWRs are too long to fit in most natural uranium reactors, notably Canada's CANDU model. Also, there may not be enough natural uranium power plants operating in the 1980s and 1990s to accommodate all the world's LWR fuel.

A variant of this idea is the spectral shift reactor. Heavy water would replace a little more than half the light (or ordinary) water used in most power reactors. This would provide a slightly faster spectrum of neutrons and increase the formation of plutonium, but it would forestall the build-up of fission products that poison the nuclear chain reaction.

Over the life of each fuel load, the heavy water would be bled down from a concentration of 60 percent to one of 10 percent, allowing most of the plutonium and U-235 to be burned. The spectral shift arrangement would require a substantial increase in U.S. heavy water production, but it would seem to demand only relatively modest hardware changes in existing power plants.[9]

Other alternatives would modify the conventional Purex reprocessing plant to make weapons-ready plutonium less accessible while allowing the plutonium and leftover uranium to be recycled in fresh fuel. In coprocessing, for instance, uranium and plutonium would be extracted together from spent fuel rather than being separated, as in military production plants, only to be later recombined. The mixture that would emerge from a reprocessing plant modified in this way would contain 1 kilogram of plutonium to 100 kilograms of slightly enriched uranium—too dilute for use in an explosive.

A government could still divert this mixture and chemically separate the plutonium, but this would require duplicating the back end of a fuel reprocessing plant, at least on a small scale. Moreover, for each weapon a diverter would have to move and process not 5 kilograms of plutonium but 500 kilograms of mixed oxide.

One advantage of coprocessing is that it would seem to require no major redesign of fuel processing plants. But to what extent it would delay a government bent on obtaining a small number of weapons is still uncertain. Equally uncertain is its applicability to breeder reactors whose fuel would need higher concentrations of plutonium.

Beyond coprocessing, U.S. and British industry researchers have proposed a recycling scheme called Civex that would leave radioactive fission products from spent fuel mixed with plutonium so that freshly fabricated, mixed-oxide fuel would subject anyone approaching it without tons of shielding and special handling equipment to lethal levels of radiation. Proponents of this concept believe that such fuel would be diversion-proof in the sense that extracting plutonium from it would demand essentially the same time and effort as reprocessing stored spent fuel.[10]

Basically, spent fuel would be reprocessed as in a Purex plant, except that the plant would not be equipped to strip a final few percent of fission products from plutonium (slightly enriched uranium could be recovered in pure form, however). Fresh fuel using the plutonium-fission product mixture would be fabricated by remote handling equipment.

The idea has been proposed by Dr. Chauncy Starr, president of the Electric Power Research Institute, the U.S. utility industry's research arm, and by Dr. Walter Marshall, deputy director of the United Kingdom Atomic Energy Authority, who contend that the Civex fuel cycle should make it possible to proceed with commercial development of breeder reactor technology on a global scale without fear of endowing countries outside the nuclear club with a nuclear weapons option. They note that fission products in the fresh fuel would probably preclude its use in existing power reactors, but that the fuel would work well in breeders. And, according to EPRI, every step in the Civex concept, including the fabrication of highly radioactive fresh fuel, has been demonstrated, at least on a laboratory scale, in the United States and Britain as part of numerous unrelated research projects carried out since the late 1950s.

Officials and analysts in the Carter administration have greeted the idea with a mixture of interest and skepticism. One point of uncertainty is the real difficulty that a government would face in modifying a Civex reprocessing plant to glean at least a few tens of kilograms of plutonium in a short time. Some authorities have also expressed concern that an unrestricted, worldwide market for Civex reprocessing and fuel fabrication plants might convey sensitive plutonium handling technology to nuclear importers and thus facilitate overt weapons programs.

Probably the most draconian solution currently under discussion—apart from simply declaring spent reactor fuel and the plutonium inside to be waste and burying it—would involve a fundamental change in commercial fission technology, largely supplanting U-238 with thorium, and U-235 and plutonium with U-233. The latter appears to be an excellent reactor fuel, but it is also a weapons material. Unlike plutonium, however, it can be diluted isotopically and denatured.

The concept of a denatured fuel cycle has been advanced most prominently by several Princeton University researchers.[11] Central to this idea is a system of internationally operated nuclear fuel centers supplying power reactors under national control. But rather than shipping a mixture of plutonium and uranium, the centers would supply fuel composed of U-233, U-238, and thorium. The U-238 would dilute the fissionable uranium to below weapons grade; the thorium would be converted into more U-233.

National power systems would return spent fuel to the international centers, where reprocessing plants would extract freshly made U-233, immediately denature it with U-238, mix it with more thorium, and send it all back in the form of new fuel. The system would not be entirely free of plutonium, as some of the U-238 diluent would be unavoidably transmuted. But quantities of plutonium from a given number of reactors would be reduced by as much as 80 percent; the remainder would stay in the international centers, where reactors would burn it to generate electricity and convert more thorium to U–233.

Advocates of the thorium alternative generally acknowledge that implementing it would entail a great deal of engineering development, the creation of a thorium mining industry (although thorium is more abundant than uranium), and an unprecedented degree of international cooperation in energy supply.

The Princeton researchers in particular caution against blind reliance on technical fixes: "One cannot wave the magic wand of a thorium cycle or some other technical innovation to make an essentially political problem turn into a technical one."[12]

Ultimately, the usefulness of any restraint on world access to plutonium for weapons may be determined by developments in the field of uranium enrichment. Any development that greatly simplified this process would render modification (or abandonment) of the plutonium cycle moot.

From the standpoint of the would-be weapons state, the ideal enrichment technology—cheap, compact, simple, and energy-efficient—does not exist. But some emerging technologies do meet some of these criteria. Among them are sophisticated laser systems that, in their early stages of development, suggest the possibility of extremely compact and efficient uranium enrichment. West Germany and South Africa have also developed new enrichment methods based on aerodynamic principles. South Africa operates a large pilot plant that may be capable of making weapons-grade uranium, and West Germany intends to sell its process—the only commercial enrichment that is unclassified and open for export—to Brazil. The sale agreement, however, stipulates construction of only one plant for low-enriched uranium.

It is too early to tell whether these developments represent serious erosion of the barriers to enrichment that have persisted since World War II. Even if these barriers are crumbling slowly, there would appear to be a consensus in the American arms control community that the task of building new ones between peaceful and military applications of plutonium is nonetheless urgent.

APPENDIX—CATEGORIES OF REACTORS

Many types of reactors have been devised over the past thirty years but the following five broad categories bear importantly on proliferation issues.

Light-Water Reactors

The predominant type of electric power reactor, the LWR burns uranium enriched with 2 to 4 percent of the fissionable isotope U-235 and uses ordinary or "light" water (H_2O) as both coolant and moderator. A moderator is a substance that slows neutrons down to improve their chances of causing U-235 atoms to fission. The main suppliers of LWRs are the United States, West Germany, and France.

Natural Uranium Reactors

The other major type of power reactor (there is roughly one for every four LWRs in the world) burns natural uranium containing 0.7 percent U-235. This eliminates the need for uranium enrichment technology but requires a more efficient moderator—either heavy water (made from deuterium, or heavy hydrogen, D_2O) or graphite. Natural uranium reactors produce about 30 percent more plutonium than LWRs of the same size. Canada is the main exporter.

High-Temperature Gas Reactors

HTGRs use helium gas as a coolant and graphite as a moderator. They run on highly enriched, weapons-grade U-235, but have the advantage of producing very little plutonium as a by-product. HTGRs can also generate a substantial part of their own fuel by converting thorium to U-233, which could be burned in place of naturally occurring U-235. Even though this would have the effect of stretching uranium resources, U-233 can also be used in explosives.

One demonstration HTGR is operating in the United States at Fort St. Vrain, Colorado; but the sole U.S. manufacturer, the General Atomic Company, has no outstanding orders for more.

Research Reactors

Nearly all of the approximately sixty research reactors in thirty countries outside the nuclear weapons states are small natural uranium or light-water reactors. The latter most commonly are a special variant of LWR notable for simple design, low power, and consumption of highly enriched, weapons-grade uranium.

Despite their small size, research reactors can be significant sources of plutonium. The only two reactors outside the weapons states that are not subject to IAEA safeguards are natural uranium research reactors. One is a forty-megawatt Indian reactor of Canadian origin that supplied plutonium for India's 1974 nuclear explosion. The other is a twenty-six-megawatt French unit that Israel operates at Dimona, in the Negev Desert, believed to have given Israel a nuclear weapons capability.

Breeder Reactors

Breeders would, if commercialized, represent a new evolutionary phase of fission technology. Unlike existing reactors, breeders would produce a net gain of fissionable fuel while generating steam for electric power. Several varieties have been proposed, but the leading technology is the Liquid Metal Fast Breeder, which would transmute a "blanket" of U-238 (placed around the core to absorb surplus neutrons) into fissionable plutonium.

Potentially, breeders could increase the burnable portion of the world's uranium resources from 1 percent at present to about 60 percent. But doing so would entail commerce in plutonium that could be diverted to weapons.

The term "fast" in the name refers not to the speed of plutonium production but to the speed of the neutrons in the breeder's core, which would not be moderated. The "liquid metal" is molten sodium coolant, a substance that does not impede neutrons.

NOTES TO CHAPTER 1

1. Albert Wohlstetter et al., *Moving Toward Life in a Nuclear Armed Crowd?* (Los Angeles: Pan Heuristics Division, Science Applications, Inc., 1976).

2. See the speech by Carl Walske, president of the Atomic Industrial Forum, at the International Conference on Nuclear Power and the Public, Geneva, 27 September 1977.

3. Plutonium production figures from Thomas H. Pigford and Kiat P. Ang, "The Plutonium Fuel Cycles," *Health Physics*, Vol. 29, (Ocotber 1975): pp. 451–468. The figure of thirty-five to forty weapons assumes 6.5 rather than 5.0 kilograms of plutonium per weapon, to account for the presence of Pu–240, which has a larger critical mass than pure Pu-239.

4. See the *IAEA Bulletin*, June 1975.

5. *IAEA Bulletin*, April 1975.

6. See Wohlstetter et al., *Moving Toward Life in a Nuclear Armed Crowd?*, Table A-1, pp. 249–256. This calculation appears to count only so-called "fissile" plutonium, a term nuclear engineers use to denote the two isotopes (Pu-239 and Pu-241) that fission most readily in light-water reactors. But all isotopes of plutonium are fissile for explosive purposes and should therefore be counted. Adding Pu-240 to this inventory estimate, and taking its larger critical mass into consideration, would raise the projected amount by about 10 percent, or 12,000 kilograms.

7. *Special Safeguards Implementation Report* (Vienna: IAEA Board of Governors, 8 June 1977), p. 8. See also the *IAEA Safeguards Technical Manual* (Vienna: IAEA-174), p. 6.

8. Special National Intelligence Estimate, September 1974 (unclassified summary released by the U.S. Department of Energy in February 1978).

9. William D. Metz, "Reprocessing Alternatives: The Options Multiply," *Science*, 15 April 1977, pp. 284–286. See also Arms Control and Disarmament Agency, Publication 91 (Washington, D.C.: GPO, December 1976).

10. Information released by the Electric Power Research Institute, Palo Alto, Calif., 27 February 1978 at the Fifth Energy Technology Conference, Washington, D.C.

11. See Ted Greenwood, Harold Feiveson, and Theodore B. Taylor, *Nuclear Proliferation: Motivations, Capabilities, and Strategies for Control,* published for the Council on Foreign Relations by McGraw-Hill, 1977. See also Taylor et al., *Bulletin of the Atomic Scientists,* December 1976.

12. Greenwood, Feiveson, and Taylor, *Nuclear Proliferation,* p. 190.

※   *Chapter 2*

Must We Decide Now
for Worldwide Commerce
in Plutonium Fuel?

Albert Wohlstetter

During 1977 the British government held a lengthy series of hearings under the Town and Country Planning Act of 1971 to review the proposal by British Nuclear Fuels Limited to establish a plant for the reprocessing of nuclear fuels at its Windscale and Calder Works on the northwestern coast of England. These formal proceedings were presided over by Justice Michael Parker. As this chapter was being written, the matter was awaiting a parliamentary review, following a finding by Justice Parker that the plant could be built. Friends of the Earth, Ltd., an intervenor in the process, had earlier invited Albert Wohlstetter to testify, and the document printed below is his prepared testimony of September 5-6, 1977 with annotations and minor corrections. The format of an English legal document has been retained, except for the paragraph numbers. References to "Day 30," etc., are to prior testimony.

Wohlstetter's testimony came at a time when he was completing the second of two major studies on the risks connected with the spread of nuclear technology, studies which have been especially influential in affecting U.S. policy. The particular value of this testimony is that it distills into a succinct and readable form a complex variety of issues and judgments that would otherwise require days of scholarly research to absorb. Because much of Wohlstetter's material was first presented in public at the California Seminar and sharpened in the course of discussions there, it is quite appropriate that the Seminar give it a wider distribution.[1]

The first three paragraphs of the original testimony consisted of a statement of qualifications of the witness in the area under consideration (see About the Authors, Albert Wohlstetter).

THE MAIN ISSUE

It is unfortunate that the issues raised by the widespread application of civilian nuclear energy are often presented to the public in the form of extreme choices: the halting and dismantling of all nuclear reactors on the one hand, or on the other, proceeding without delay to a commitment to commerce in forms of civilian nuclear power, nuclear services, and nuclear research activities which would make plutonium or highly enriched uranium widely accessible to many governments and quickly usable in nuclear explosives. These extremes tend to feed on each other. Unless there is an earnest endeavor at moderation in the views and behavior of the nuclear industry and of government offices concerned with nuclear energy, as well as in the views and behavior of their critics, we may have to look forward to increased polarization and violent confrontations of the sort occurring recently in Germany and France. In any case these extremes do not represent the genuine alternatives available.

I believe that some forms of nuclear electric power are comparatively safe, and that they will play a useful role in the generation of electricity. The studies in which my colleagues and I have been engaged, however, show that some other forms of nuclear electric power — and in particular some that have had no commercial significance as yet but that have been long contemplated as destined to become commonplace — are plainly dangerous. Their widespread application would increase the likelihood of an extensive and rapid spread of nuclear weapons to many countries that do not at present have them. We have also found, however, that delaying for several years the decision for unrestricted commerce in these dangerous technologies, services, materials, and facilities would impose no significant economic sacrifice or loss of scarce resources. We find that it is likely to save rather than lose money and that it would give time to the international community to develop safer arrangements.

Considerations of this sort led to the change in U.S. policy announced by President Ford on October 28, 1976 and affirmed and expanded by President Carter on April 7, 1977. However, these arguments apply not only to the United States, as is sometimes claimed, but to the other industrial countries and to the less developed world. The real issues lie between those who insist that an immediate commitment to this dangerous commerce is essential and urgent, and those who hold that there is time to think freshly about the alternatives and to design a new set of international conventions on the use and export of nuclear energy to replace or supplement the arrangements worked out in the Nonproliferation Treaty (NPT). In particular the main issue in contention at this inquiry appears to be between those on the one hand who claim that there is no feasible alternative other than to proceed now with an investment in a greatly expanded facility for separating plutonium from spent uranium oxide fuel, and to help finance this investment by contracting to supply services to separate plutonium for governments that have no nuclear weapons, and those, on the other hand, who say that delaying this drastic step is both feasible, prudent, and in fact demanded by the complexity of the decisions in which the British government will have to participate in the next few years.

The great difficulty facing political leaders in these decisions is that the issues are not only complicated but also involve a mixture of many professional disciplines and kinds of experience: not only physics, chemistry, nuclear engineering, weapons design, and geology, but also economics, operational research, systems analysis, and a wide range of international political-military considerations. No single person can be taken to be an expert in all of these fields. But unfortunately, since experts do not come precisely labeled as to their contents, like drugs or other pharmaceuticals, a political leader tends to be at the mercy of judgments that quite innocently may extend beyond the actual knowledge and experience of those informing him. And this inescapable problem can be intensified by any false urgency that rushes decision before there has been an adequate airing of the considerations involved. Decisions on nuclear technology have been particularly vulnerable because of the prevalent secrecy about the materials and designs of nuclear weapons. Much secrecy is plainly essential if we are to slow the spread of nuclear weapons, but some has been counterproductive for that very purpose. To give one important example, misinformation and confusion about the possibility of denaturing fissile material and the supposed impossibility of using power reactor plutonium in military explosives was widespread enough to mislead statesmen for the very beginnings of the Atoms for Peace programs. Though a substantial amount of information has been released, especially in the last year, the illusion that power reactor plutonium cannot be used in an "effective weapon," and that no country may use it "to become in any sense a nuclear power," continues, it seems, to confuse the issues in contention at this inquiry (see, for example, Day 30, 26 July, p. 77). Such misinformation has had an effect in my own country as well as in England, and perhaps especially in countries like the Federal Republic of Germany which has no military nuclear energy program.

It appears to me, for example, that the information supplied to Chancellor Schmidt by his technical experts has sometimes been seriously lacking not only on the military implications, but on the disposal of radioactive wastes and on the economics of plutonium and uranium. Nonetheless, Schmidt himself recently made a very wise and balanced statement on the subject of nuclear proliferation which implies that it is going to take a substantial time and effort to develop a new system of international conventions to deal with the dangers. He said:

> President Carter was right to set before world opinion the extremely complicated problems of the peaceful use of nuclear energy. The development of this form of energy is such and the technical innovations are so numerous that the provisions of the nonproliferation treaty are no longer sufficient to guarantee nuclear plants against military use. The United States is trying to ward off this danger by establishing a world system of contractual ties, and the FRG Government will certainly cooperate in this effort.[2]

Chancellor Schmidt recognizes that "the system which must be developed will be extremely complicated, given the number and diversity of the state(s) involved."

The problem of preventing or at least slowing and limiting the further spread of nuclear weapons is clearly a complicated one. An adequate program must deal with highly enriched uranium as well as plutonium and with research reactors and critical experiments as well as power reactors, and it should aim to improve the bilaterial and international inspection systems. Moreover, such a program must concern itself not only with restrictions on these sensitive materials, facilities, and services, but also with providing safer substitutes for them at minimal economic sacrifice and on a nondiscriminatory basis. Finally, it must deal with the structure of alliances and guarantees that may keep incentives low for countries to acquire nuclear weapons in their own defense. Nonetheless, restrictions on commerce in sensitive materials, facilities, and services are a necessary though not sufficient condition for any serious program to slow and limit the spread of nuclear weapons.

ARGUMENTS FOR AN IMMEDIATE
COMMITMENT TO PLUTONIUM FUEL

Almost everyone who advocates an immediate commitment to commerce in plutonium fuel, either for burner or for breeder reactors, pays his respects to the goal of nonproliferation, and the improvement of "safeguards." This is certainly true in my own country for representatives of the Atomic Industrial Forum, the American Nuclear Society, the Electric Power Research Institute, all four major reactor manufacturers, as well as those firms which have invested in the separation of plutonium. The impressive list of members of the Atomic Industrial Forum's Committee on Nuclear Export Policy has stated that we should promote peaceful electric power only to the extent consistent with the goal of eliminating proliferation.[3] I observe that the witnesses of British Nuclear Fuels Limited (BNFL) who have appeared at this inquiry have also made a bow in the direction of improving "safeguards" and conforming to the requirements of the Nonproliferation Treaty (NPT) not in any way to assist governments without nuclear weapons to acquire them.

However, like the Forum's Committee on Nuclear Export Policy, the representatives of BNFL and the U.K. Department of Energy suggest that the export of such services and commodities as plutonium separation or plutonium dioxide would not significantly assist governments that do not have nuclear weapons to get them; that a country which is determined to arm itself with nuclear weapons will get them in any case, and will not be prevented by a prohibition on its separating plutonium nor, it is implied, on its importing separated plutonium from other countries.[4] This argument is presented in much expanded form in the United States by various advocates of an immediate commitment to plutonium fuel, who obligingly list several alternative paths to nuclear weapons material, which they claim are even shorter, easier, and cheaper than the path starting with separated power reactor plutonium.[5] The straightest, shortest path, we are told, is simply to get a production reactor and separation facilities overtly "dedicated" to producing and separating plutonium for weapons.

Representatives of BNFL suggest that Article IV of the NPT obligates the British government to supply separation services and that the Americans may be influenced in arguing the need to delay to devise alternatives to the use of plutonium fuel by the fact that the United States (and Canada and Australia) have more uranium than other countries and are therefore rather more careless than other industrial countries and the Third World about the attractions of an immediate commitment to plutonium for achieving energy independence. They suggest also that a government depending on nuclear power and denied the "fruits of reprocessing" by other countries (i.e. separated plutonium) might feel compelled to build separation plants of their own, even if guarantees are given them of a continuing supply of slightly enriched uranium.[6] On the other hand, they suggest that further assurance against the misuse of separated plutonium can be achieved by international storage and close control of the separated plutonium. And finally, even if a delay in reprocessing might save money and cannot mean any significant loss of money or scarce resources, BNFL believes that the need to dispose of radioactive waste will in any case dictate the reprocessing of spent uranium oxide fuel, and that the direct disposal of spent uranium oxide fuel rods is not an acceptable course (point 18 of the Statement of Submissions of BNFL).

SUMMARY OF ANSWERS TO THE ARGUMENTS
FOR IMMEDIATE COMMITMENT

First, there are, of course, other paths to nuclear weapons than those that start with separated power reactor plutonium in the form, say, of plutonium dioxide. On the conventions as to what has been legitimate civilian activity up to now, some of these paths might even start with the large quantities of plutonium and highly enriched uranium in metal form sometimes used in critical experiments. From such a starting point the remainder of the way to a nuclear explosive material ready for incorporation in a bomb would be even shorter. Other paths, starting with the construction of a simple production reactor, are not, as claimed, easier and more direct than the path starting with separated power-reactor plutonium and I will comment on that at greater length. However, the intention of President Carter's proposal is plainly to develop international agreements blocking essentially all such plausible routes and not just one. To argue, as do those who want immediate commitments to unrestricted commerce in separated plutonium from power reactors, that such restrictions would be irrelevant because there are other ways to get a bomb is like opposing innoculation for smallpox because one might also die of bubonic plague. Better to suggest protection against the plague as well. The argument that any determined country can get nuclear weapons in any event and in even less time and at less cost than through the use of separated power reactor plutonium scarcely fits with the advocates' argument that there is some point in improving inspection systems. It sometimes seems that extreme advocates of immediate commitment to plutonium are busily supplying arguments for the opposite extreme, which holds that all forms of nuclear energy are too dangerous and should all be banned.

Second, bilateral and international inspection systems do indeed need improvement but if such improved inspection is to be more than a facade for a possible steady advance toward nuclear explosive materials by states that do not presently have them, the facilities, processes, and stocks inspected must be far enough away from yielding bomb material to make timely warning feasible. Some of the processes that have been contemplated in the use of plutonium as fuel, as well as in the conduct of critical experiments, would be too close even if inspection were infallible and instantaneous. (See, for example, the analyses by some colleagues, qualified by training and long experience in chemical reprocessing, of the production of plutonium metal either from plutonium nitrate or plutonium oxide and of the separation of plutonium nitrate from fresh mixed oxide fuel[7]). Unless such sensitive technologies are restricted, "effective safeguards" in the sense defined by the IAEA for the NPT are literally infeasible.

Third, the economic prospects for the use of plutonium rather than fresh uranium fuel in light-water reactors have worsened drastically. The estimated costs for separating plutonium have multiplied over tenfold in little more than a decade. They have in fact, even allowing for inflation in the general price level, jumped by a factor of nearly seven in two years, between the U.S. AEC estimate of $30 per kilogram of spent fuel in 1974 and the estimate of $280 in mid-1976 by its successor agency, ERDA.

In the negotiations between COGEMA and JAPCO, the price of separating a kilogram has been reported to range up to $700 and as high as $400 in constant 1977 dollars.[a] On lower estimates by my colleagues, the future costs of plutonium fuel still exceed those of fresh uranium. Plutonium advocates disagree, and, of course, both our and their estimates are quite uncertain. However, the area of agreement is less in doubt and more important, namely, that even on the most optimistic estimates recycling of plutonium in light-water reactors can make only a slight difference in the costs of a delivered kilowatt hour. Fuel cycle costs are only one-tenth of delivered costs of electricity, and recycling can displace only a fraction of the fuel cycle costs; the total savings would be at most only 1 or 2 percent, even if plutonium separation were costless. (The economics of plutonium fuel in burner reactors is of importance for these hearings even if the United Kingdom itself does not contemplate such use. They will certainly affect long-term commercial prospects for the business of selling a service of separating uranium oxide for the world market.)

However, if we remind ourselves that the main issue is whether to defer decision or commit ourselves now to plutonium fuel, the area of disagreement is smaller still. On the analysis of the Final Generic Environmental Statement on Mixed-Oxide Fuel in mid-1976, advocates of an immediate commitment on the staff of the U.S. Nuclear Regulatory Commission estimated that a five-year delay would cost $74 million in discounted 1975 dollars over a 25-year period; and a

---

[a]In December 1977, after the presentation of this testimony, the price set by COGEMA in its contract with German utilities was reported to be $500 per kilogram in constant 1977 dollars. The $500 price charged by COGEMA, moreover, applies to reprocessing in the new large facility with a capacity of 1,600 MTU per year, planned for completion at Cap de la Hague in the late 1980s.[8] Evidence presented by BNFL at these hearings indicates a cost of 260 pounds sterling ($460) per kilogram in mid-1977 pounds sterling, though the evidence was not clear or detailed enough for this figure to be firm.

ten-year delay $300 million.[b] These sums are very small compared to the discounted sums that would be invested in the nuclear fuel cycle and in reactors during that period. The advocates' own reckoning implies that the cost of a five-year delay would be measured in hundredths of 1 percent of the cost of a delivered kilowatt hour of electricity. Even a ten-year delay would add less than a tenth of 1 percent to delivered kilowatt hour costs. In the light of the long and disastrous history of failures in predicting nuclear costs, demand, and supply, it would take a heroic faith to assign any reality, much less any importance, to such small differences.

On the other hand, since investment expenditures are made early and benefits received much later, premature commitment can mean a very large financial penalty in the event of failures. That penalty may be passed along to foreign or domestic utilities or borne by the manufacturer, but ultimately it will be borne by taxpayers or users of electricity. Such economic arguments apply even more forcefully to the Third World countries that contemplate reprocessing, since they would experience much higher costs through the diseconomies of small scale. The political and military penalties imposed by early commitment to separating plutonium are even larger and some may be substantially irreversible.

Fourth, the conservation benefits must be related to the economics. The supply of uranium worth finding and extracting is, of course, a function of expected price. Whether we extract plutonium from spent uranium fuel or mine fresh uranium ore depends on future relative costs that are very uncertain. Our estimates show that plutonium fuel would cost more than it is worth. But the fact that the mining and milling costs of uranium oxide are only half the fuel cycle costs and thus about 5 percent of the delivered kilowatt-hour costs, suggests that the price of uranium yellowcake, or U_3O_8, could rise by a large factor without prohibitive effects on the costs of electricity. Plutonium in light-water reactors can displace at most a modest fraction of uranium fuel, that will vary among other things with the assumed rate of growth of nuclear electric power. The more rapid the rate of growth and the consequent demand for nuclear fuel, the smaller the fraction of fresh uranium fuel it can displace. Thus in various projections it has been estimated to save between 10 and 25 percent.

For the purposes of this inquiry the issue is a narrower one. How much would uranium conservation be affected by a delay of five or ten years in a commitment to plutonium? The answer is very little.

---

[b]Though described at the hearings as a five- or ten-year delay, a rereading of the text cited indicates that the periods of time were eight and thirteen years, respectively, thus reinforcing this point.

If the spent uranium fuel is placed in retrievable storage, as it would be, nearly all the fissile plutonium would be there ready for use if desired, since some 85 percent of it is plutonium-239 with a half-life of about 24,000 years. The 15 percent is constituted by plutonium-241, which has a thirteen-year half-life. As a result after five years, 96 percent, and after ten years 94 percent of the total fissile plutonium would remain. That would mean that if previously the plutonium were going to displace 20 percent of the uranium, it would then be able to displace only about 19 percent. On the other hand, the spent uranium would have cooled meanwhile, making it somewhat less expensive to reprocess.

Fifth, stocks of plutonium or other highly concentrated fissile material might be used for initial loadings of fast breeders. However, this is not a very convincing reason for expanding Windscale now. Whether the fast plutonium breeder will ever be an economic way to produce fissile material is highly uncertain, depending not only on many technical developments, but on the future capital costs of various breeder and burner reactors; the reprocessing costs of such intensely irradiated fuel; the future price of fresh uranium; the growth in demand for electricity; the reserve electric generating capacity, and many other variables. Even if it should become economic, still more uncertain are the date at which it would become so, and the realistic rate and extent at which it might grow in commercial significance, without risk of losing enormous investments. I am not closely familiar with the British fast-breeder program but I observe that, like the U.S. and other breeder programs, it has been slipping. Since the much faster schedule submitted in 1974–1975 by the United Kingdom AEA to the Royal Commission on Environmental Pollution, Mr. Blumfield of the Dounreay Experimental Research Establishment is reported as testifying that the commercial breeders are not likely to be ordered until sixteen to eighteen years after an order is placed for CFR–1.[9] This would mean that orders for commercial breeders would not be made until 1993–1995, with commercial introduction near the year 2000, and about 30 GWe of commercial breeders on-line in 2010. Initial loadings for such a schedule would not appear to require an immediate expansion of oxide reprocessing at Windscale. The plutonium supplied from the reprocessing of magnox fuel should supply breeder needs at least until the year 2000. In the United States at any rate, which I believe has smaller civilian stocks of plutonium than the United Kingdom, initial breeder loadings have been found to be no justification for early reprocessing. My statement will end with some remarks on chronic premature commitment in the nuclear industry and its penalties. I will include there some comments on the record of breeder predictions and its implications for sensible strategies of decision.

Sixth, it is part of President Carter's program to work out assurances that slightly enriched uranium fuel will be available on a non-discriminatory basis to meet the fuel demands of countries that observe the new conventions against proliferation. Some of the reasons making this feasible are that the demand for nuclear electric power and therefore, the derived demand for nuclear fuel have been greatly exaggerated and have now been scaled down drastically. The outlook for supply at a reasonable price is good for the rest of the century. Moreover, since fresh slightly enriched uranium fuel is not an explosive material, it should be possible to arrange for substantial working stocks under effective national control. The program is also made feasible by the fact that fuel costs are relatively small in proportion to investment costs and since the fuel is not bulky, storage costs are not excessive.

Representatives of BNFL, however, suggest as an alternative to dependence on slightly enriched uranium, that those governments (which are supposedly moved by a concern for "energy independence" to obtain the conservation benefits of plutonium) be allowed to purchase plutonium, but that the plutonium be placed under strict international storage and control and released only according to international criteria. This proposal would make these countries more rather than less dependent on outside sources for an uninterrupted fuel supply, and their reactor operations would be much more liable to shut-downs than with the slightly enriched uranium fuel it would be feasible and safe to supply. Presumably, BNFL's proposal would mean keeping strategic quantities of plutonium out of the hands of governments that do not have nuclear weapons. If such arrangements were practicable at all, keeping the amount of plutonium under national control to less than a bomb's worth or a few bombs' worth would allow these countries almost no working stocks of mixed plutonium and uranium oxide (MOX) or separated plutonium under their own control. With only one MOX reload as a working stock for each reactor, and assuming they do not fabricate their own MOX fuel, in the 1990s Japan and the Federal Republic of Germany would each have more than 1,000 bombs' worth of plutonium quickly accessible and even Spain would have 650 bombs' worth. (That is, on their plans up to recently. If they fabricated their own MOX fuel they would have even more plutonium, in forms still more directly used in nuclear weapons.) But less than one thousandth, or one 650th, of a country's annual reload requirement could hardly be called a working stock.

The American experience with India offers strong evidence that even supplies of slightly enriched uranium fuel that would have been enough to guarantee operation of the Tarapur reactor for over two years have been deemed by the Indian government to be below emergency levels, dictating resupply by air and other speedy action. Moreover, the debate in the 1950s on the draft of the IAEA Statute focused on similar though less drastic proposals for deposit of fissionable materials with the IAEA. Even then it was made clear that to give such powers to the IAEA was unacceptable to governments like India, as threatening their economic life and their independence.[c] It seems extremely unlikely that governments trying to secure a little more energy independence by the use of plutonium fuel than if the they used only natural or slightly enriched uranium would accept a new international institution depriving them of any significant national control of such plutonium, thus making them more rather than less dependent on outside powers for continuity of supply.

Fresh low enriched uranium stocks under national control are more likely to be susceptible to limitations satisfying both the user's desire for adequate working stocks and the international community's desire to keep stocks of highly concentrated fissionable material out of the hands of nonweapon states. It is also true that international control and close, even continuous, inspection of spent uranium fuel would intrude much less into the essential operation of power or research reactors, yet serve an important function in providing early warning of diversion.

Seventh, the rather unqualified statement in point 18 of the BNFL Statement of Submissions that the direct disposal of spent uranium fuel is "not an acceptable course" certainly runs counter to the body of professional opinion in the United States and in Canada and Sweden, including the opinion of those who on other grounds favor the use of plutonium fuel. I am not an expert in radioactive waste management but some of my colleagues are and I have followed their work. In Canada and in the United States and Sweden, professional judgment accepts the view that permanent disposal of radioactive wastes is likely best to be achieved by geologic isolation in stable formations such as bedded salt or granite and that this would apply

---

[c]Dr. Bhabha rejected the draft proposal which gave the IAEA the power "to approve the means to be used for chemical processing of irradiated materials recovered or produced as a by-product, and to require that such special fissionable materials be deposited with the Agency except for quantities authorized by the Agency to be retained for specified non-military use under continuing Agency safeguards."[10] "In our opinion," Dr. Bhabha continued, "the present draft gives the Agency the power to interfere in the economic life of States which come to it for aid. . . .It therefore constitutes a threat to their independence, which will be greater in proportion to the extent that this atomic power generation is developed through Agency aid."[11]

both to the solidified and vitrified reprocessed waste and to the stainless steel-clad or zirconium alloy-clad ceramic uranium oxide pellets. For example, this conclusion is stated by Erik Svenke, Managing Director of the Swedish Nuclear Fuel Supply Company and member of AKA, the Swedish Government Committee on Radioactive Waste. In a June 1976 lecture at the IAEA in Vienna, Svenke summarized the Committee's findings that "if reprocessing and reuse is not to be implemented, the commission is convinced that a safe terminal storage of spent fuel can be developed as well."[12] In the United States the Final Generic Environmental Statement on Mixed-Oxide Fuel (GESMO) of August 1976 concluded as a result of the most complete study of geological containment failure mechanisms in bedded salt and their consequences that a serious breach of containment is an extremely remote possibility. Even the surface burst of a large (50 megaton) nuclear weapon could not breach the containment, once the repository had been sealed. From the standpoint of permanent disposal, it found no clear preference as between the direct disposal of spent uranium and the disposal of reprocessed, recycled, and vitrified wastes.[13]

The work of colleagues indicates that on the safety criteria used in the United States, the volume and heat content of the waste created by reprocessing and by the irradiation of MOX fuel that requires remote handling and geologic isolation are somewhat larger than those for the direct disposal of spent uranium fuel. In the case of the Federal Republic of Germany and Sweden, this difference would be still larger, since their standards are even more rigorous, requiring the geological isolation even of low-level waste.[14] German experts continue to contemplate storing reprocessed waste rather than direct disposal, but the advantage in volume required for direct disposal of spent uranium has some bearing on the concern expressed by Chancellor Schmidt that small countries might have to worry more about the space taken up by radioactive waste than a large country like the United States. Even though the total volumes involved are not very large in either case, it appears they are larger for the reprocessed fuel.

These hearings have referred to the studies of Dr. Katayama of Battelle Pacific Northwest Laboratories showing that the caesium leach rate of irradiated LWR fuel pellets is roughly the same as that of borosilicate glass, the most leach resistant of the materials considered for glassifying reprocessed waste. Dr. Katayama has also assured my colleagues working on the waste problem that this result applies not only to caesium, which is the most leachable of the elements in the waste, but in approximately the same way to the cumulative leaching of all the other elements in the waste as well.[d]

However, the main question at issue here as to waste disposal is not to decide the very long-term question of geologic isolation. It is, once again a narrower issue: whether it is urgent for the United Kingdom to commit itself now to reprocessing as a mode of waste disposal or whether it can afford to wait for several years before finally deciding between direct disposal of the spent fuel or disposing of it after reprocessing. Here I think the answer is quite clear.

I have not seen the testimony of Mr. John Wright of the Central Electricity Generating Board (CEGB). He is, however, quoted in the August 18, 1977 *Nucleonics Week* as saying, "The CEGB's anxiety is that if Thorp were not built and fuel were returned for storage for an indefinite period, it is conceivable that after ten years the oxide fuel could undergo sudden and rapid deterioration, giving rise to acute activity and handling problems." If this occurs, according to *Nucleonics Week*, BNFL might not accept any more spent AGR fuel and all the AGRs in England would have to shut down for ten years while a reprocessing plant was built. Mr. Wright considers this an unacceptable risk for the CEGB.

Perhaps Mr. Wright's concern can be diminished, if not laid to rest, by the citation of some relevant American experience reported by ERDA in May 1975,[16] which indicated that both stainless steel and zirconium alloy-clad irradiated fuel had been stored in water-filled basins for periods up to ten years and that the corrosion rates for both had been extremely low during these ten years. The effects of corrosion after extremely long storage times, on the order of 100 years, may need to be examined further, the publication says. However, there is always the alternative of storage in air-cooled vaults which could be readied for operation in seven to nine years,[17] and ERDA points out that architectural use of stainless steel for the last thirty years has resulted in little corrosion.

The upshot of this evidence is to suggest that a "sudden and rapid deterioration" of the stainless steel cladding of the AGR fuel through

---

[d](Footnote added after September 5 testimony.) In any case the leachability of spent LWR fuel compared to that of the vitrified reprocessed waste would be of primary importance in considering the permanent disposition of such waste only if such manmade structures were intended to be the primary permanent barrier between the waste and man. Indeed the U.K. Atomic Energy Authority once appeared so to regard them when it planned to dump vitrified waste directly into the ocean. However, it is very doubtful that any such manmade structure will last for the extended period contemplated on the phrase "permanent disposal."[15] For final disposal the primary barrier now contemplated between radioactive waste and man would be geologic isolation in some formation that has been stable for millions of years, such as bedded salt or granite or some deep layers of the ocean bed.

some unknown and hence uspecified mechanism does not appear to be a very serious danger, at least not one comparable to dangers from the spread of plutonium explosive material worldwide. Some of this stainless steel-clad fuel in the United States has been stored in a pool for twelve years (the fuel from the Vallecitos Boiling Water Reactor of General Electric).[e]

In short, given the serious consequences, some of which may be irreversible, of the spread of plutonium, deferring this decision to expand Windscale seems only prudent. None of the reasons advanced for rushing to decision can sustain examination.

SOME POINTS REQUIRING EXTENDED STATEMENT

My remaining points, I fear, require a less summary exposition. In all of the above, I have assumed that the separated plutonium from power reactors that the United Kingdom may contract to separate and export to countries without nuclear weapons can be used by the government laboratories of such states to make implosion devices

---

[e](Footnote added after September 5 testimony) During the hearings at Whitehaven Mr. Justice Parker asked BNFL to study the condition of the spent AGR fuel it has stored in pools. Evidence produced by this necessarily hasty study indicates that the AGR fuel may suffer corrosion resulting in pinhole leaks after only five years. This evidence is uncertain, not only because the study was hurried, but also because BNFL's records on pool storage of AGR fuel elements are admittedly incomplete in some essentials. The corrosion that has occurred up to now is being managed by normal pool storage techniques. The rate of further corrosion, its causes, and whether its further effects can be managed without resorting to special storage techniques are also uncertain. If they cannot, this would not mean that spent AGR fuel must be reprocessed. For the future the problem might be avoided, for example, by redesign of the cladding, using perhaps a nickel chromium alloy. For the smaller quantities of spent AGR fuel currently stored in pools, BNFL recognizes that the changes in chemistry of the pool water may greatly reduce the corrosion rate. If these measures are inadequate, the spent AGR fuel might be stored, for example, in helium-filled or water-filled stainless steel containers. While such a measure would entail an increase in costs, this increase would be small compared to the costs associated with the expansion of Windscale, not to say the distribution of plutonium worldwide.

The United Kingdom is the only country that uses British advanced gas-cooled reactors, so AGR fuel problems would not form the basis for a world market for separation services to overcome them; and therefore the expansion of Windscale could not be justified on that account. The hasty study by BNFL confirmed the results of a recent more extended study by Battelle Pacific Northwest Laboratories,[18] which found that both zircaloy and stainless steel-clad spent fuel from water-cooled reactors have up to now suffered no corrosion in the course of storage in water pools. Both studies conclude that LWR and HWR fuels can be stored for at least twenty years. In fact, even the special problems of British magnox fuel (which can be reprocessed in existing British facilities) need not from the standpoint of waste management be solved by reprocessing.[19]

which would indeed be genuine and extremely formidable nuclear weapons, even if they used only simple designs of the kind first hit upon by the United States during the Manhattan project. Advocates of plutonium in 1976 frequently denied this. But near the end of last year, quite precise quantitative information was released covering some aspects of how the probability distribution of nuclear yields changes with the isotopic composition of the plutonium used, which in turn varies with the period of fuel irradiation.[20] This information makes clear that with power reactor-grade plutonium, an implosion weapon of even the simple design first used by the United States would reliably have yields between 1 and 20 kilotons: a most formidable military weapon, for example, against population centers of a nonnuclear adversary.

One might have hoped that the release of this quantitative information would settle the debate that had been carried on up to then in vague qualitative terms. However, some statements made at these hearings in Whitehaven disappoint that hope, as do many of the statements made since last November by representatives of the nuclear industry in the United States and in Germany. Rather than repeat what I have already said in some detail in a prior publication, I will place the relevant sections in the record at this point and comment only on a few points that have been made prominently by plutonium advocates since the release of this information.[f]

> ... A nonweapon country can operate a power reactor so as to produce significant quantities of rather pure plutonium-239 without violating any agreements, or incurring substantial extra expense. This would involve departing from theoretical "norms" for reactor operation, but a look at the actual operating record of reactors in less developed countries suggests how theoretical these norms are. Even in America in the early 1970s, leaking fuel rods caused Commonwealth Edison to discharge the initial core of its Dresden-2 reactor early, with nearly 100 bombs-worth of 89 to 95 percent pure fissile plutonium.[g] (In India, as of September, 1975, 97 percent of the fuel discharged from its Tarapur reactors had leaked.) Countries like Pakistan and India, with smaller electric grids and poorer maintenance have operated much less and much more irregularly than the steady 80 percent of the time originally hoped for: and have irradiated their fuel and contaminated the plutonium in it less. Since it is neither illegal nor uncommon to operate reactors uneconomically, governments may derive quite pure plutonium-239 with no violation nor much visibility.

---

[f]"Spreading the Bomb Without Quite Breaking the Rules," *Foreign Policy*, No. 25 (Winter 1976-77): 158-163; © 1975, reprinted with permission of Albert Wohlstetter.

[g]The spent fuel had 13 kg of plutonium that was 95 percent, 110 kg that was 93 percent, and 331 kg that was 89 percent purely fissile.

What is more, there is plainly a considerable latitude in the degree of purity actually required for explosives. The discussion in the European nuclear industry frequently assumes that "weapons-grade" plutonium must be 98 percent pure plutonium-239.[21] In this country, however, under present classification guidance, the fact that plutonium containing up to and including 8 percent plutonium-240 *is* used in weapons is unclassified as is the fact that more than 8 percent plutonium-240 (reactor-grade) *can* be used to make nuclear weapons.

Most significantly, 20 years of Atoms for Peace programs have dispersed well-equipped and well-staffed nuclear laboratories among nonnuclear weapons states throughout the world. (For example, by 1974 the United States alone had trained 1,100 Indian nuclear physicists and engineers. The shah of Iran plans to have 10,000 trained.) Many of these laboratories would be quite capable of designing and constructing an implosion device and of studying its behavior by nonnuclear firings. It is true that if they were to use power reactor plutonium with 20 to 30 percent of the higher isotopes, they would be likely to obtain a lower expected yield and a greater variation in possible yields than if they should use more nearly pure plutonium-239. (Of course a nonnuclear component could fail, but this has nothing to do with the grade of plutonium used.) However, they could build a device which, even at its lowest yield level, would produce a very formidable explosion. This may be seen from the record (now public) of the characteristics of the Nagasaki plutonium bomb.

The Fat Man and the Little Boy

The first American implosion design, "Fat Man," was used in the Trinity test and the Nagasaki bomb. It had a finite probability of predetonating even though it used an extremely high percentage of plutonium-239. Plutonium-239 itself emits neutrons spontaneously, though five orders of magnitude less so than an equal quantity of plutonium-240. More important, though the Trinity and Nagasaki devices used exceptionally pure plutonium-239, they had a significant fraction of plutonium-240. They had a definite chance, then, of detonating prematurely, that is, between the time the rapidly assembling fissile material first became critical and the time that it might have arrived at the desired degree of supercriticality; and the less supercritical, the lower the yield.

In a memorandum to General Farrell and Captain Parsons immediately after the Trinity test, and before the use of Fat Man at Nagasaki, Oppenheimer wrote, "As a result of the Trinity shot we are led to expect a very similar performance from the first Little Boy (the gun-assembled uranium weapon used at Hiroshima) and the first plutonium Fat Man. The energy release of both of these units should be in the range of 12,000 to 20,000 tons and the blast should be equivalent to that from 8,000 to 15,000 tons of TNT. The possibilities of a less than optimal performance of the Little Boy are quite small and should be ignored. The possiblity that the first combat plutonium Fat Man will give a less than optimal performance is about 12 percent. There is about a 6 percent chance that the energy release will be under 5,000 tons, and about a 2 percent chance that it will be under 1,000 tons. *It should not be much less than 1,000 tons unless there is an actual malfunctioning of some of the components. . . ."* (Italics added)[22]

Indeed General Groves, like Oppenheimer writing between the Trinity test and the actual use of the implosion weapon at Nagasaki, anticipated an increase in the fraction of plutonium-240 in later weapons. He wrote, "There is a definite possibility, 12 percent rising to 20 percent as we increase our rate of production at the Hanford Engineer Works, with the type of weapons tested that the blast will be smaller due to detonation in advance of the optimum time. *But in any event, the explosion should be on the order of thousands of tons.* The difficulty arises from an undesirable isotope which is created in greater quantity as the production rate increases." (Italics added)[23]

The essential point to be made is that even if a device like our first plutonium weapon were detonated as prematurely as possible—at a time when the fissile material was least supercritical—its yield would still be in the kiloton range. Apart from a modest degradation in the quality of the fissile material employed, and hence in the size of the expected yield, all that a higher fraction of plutonium-240 in such a first implosion device could do is increase the probability of obtaining a yield smaller than the optimal, but still as large or larger than that already enormously destructive minimum.

The lowest yield of such a weapon can by no stretch of the imagination be called "weak." Moreover, by comparison with the average or even the maximum yield possible in that implosion design (or by any standard), it would by no means be contemptible. In fact, only 7 months before Trinity, the first implosion weapons were expected to yield much *less* than one kt.[24] A reduced yield would not mean a proportionate reduction in damage. The area destroyed by blast overpressure diminishes as the two-thirds power of the reduction in yield, and the reduction in prompt radiation—which is the dominant effect on population of a low-yield weapon—is even smaller. (If the expected yield were eight kilotons, and the less probable but actual yield were "merely" one kiloton, the blast area would be reduced not by seven-eighths, but only by three-fourths and the region in which persons in residential buildings would receive a lethal dose of prompt radiation would only be halved.) The lethal area would still be nearly a square mile.

Variability in yield would be a drawback for an advanced industrial country preparing the sort of force I have referred to as of interest to an industrial power like Japan in the 1980s or 1990s. Such a power might want a theater weapon that minimized collateral damage if only for the protection of its own troops. However, for a last resort weapon used against a distant population, it is important only that the lower bound of the yield be formidable; and if in fact more destructive energy is released than anticipated, this would only reinforce the destruction intended.

Finally, the variations in damage due to differences in the purity of the plutonium are likely to be much less than the variation in damage due to the differing operational circumstances in the use of the weapon. The Nagasaki plutonium implosion bomb had an estimated yield of 21 kilotons. The Hiroshima uranium gun weapon is now estimated to have released 14 kilotons. Yet, due to differences in terrain, weather, accuracy of delivery, and the distribution of population, the Hiroshima bomb killed twice as many people as the Nagasaki weapon.

As for the argument that military men would never use a device whose result was not precisely predictable, this is not very persuasive. If so, military men would hardly ever enter battle. The uncertainties of surviving ground attack, of penetrating air defense, and of delivering weapons on target are cumulatively larger than the uncertainties in the yield of a bomb made with power-reactor plutonium. Plans for delivering the first nuclear weapons were going forward before any test, and during a period when the Manhattan Project scientists had highly varied estimates of their yield.

In sum, no one should believe that power-reactor plutonium can be used only in a feeble device too unreliable to be considered a military weapon, or that recycling plutonium is therefore safe.

The passages quoted above were intended to answer the qualitative arguments then current. Let us consider some new and some persistent confusions.

At the meeting of the American Nuclear Society and the Atomic Industrial Forum at which their members and foreign government and industry representatives had been briefed by Dr. Selden, of Lawrence Livermore Laboratories, some members of the industry held a press conference which appears to have been intended as a counter. At that press conference it was stated that, whatever the facts about the usability of reactor grade plutonium in a nuclear explosive, no country had ever used it. Since that time, this statement has been repeated in the U.S. Congress and elsewhere by leading advocates of the plutonium breeder. Now, even if true, it would hardly be relevant. (It is true, for example, that no country has yet used uranium highly enriched by a laser as bomb material, but no one doubts that should such lasers become widely available, it might well be so used.)

First, this assertion is simply false. While the exact details are classified, I am able to say that the United States, for example, has exploded a device using reactor grade plutonium. Second, this argument, especially as recently formulated, is even more meaningless than I have so far suggested, since "reactor grade plutonium" simply means plutonium that has been produced by long irradiation periods and as a result has a higher plutonium-240 and -242 content.

As I have pointed out in the article previously quoted at length, even light-water reactors characteristically operate irregularly and not at all in accordance with theoretical norms, and therefore have not infrequently discharged "weapons grade" plutonium. Moreover, since this argument has been mustered in defense of the military safety of the liquid metal fast breeder reactor, its relevance is even more obscure: the radial blankets of such reactors will *normally* contain hundreds of kilograms of "weapons grade" plutonium on discharge. In fact, they will contain 96 percent pure plutonium-239, which is considerably purer than the 92 percent limit used in the definition of "weapons grade."

In the last year, plutonium advocates have taken the newly public quantitative information in their stride by suggesting that the yield would be "only" a few kilotons. Since the aim of the entire Manhattan Project was to get a yield of one kiloton, and since seven months before the first nuclear test, its leaders expected the yield to be considerably less, and nevertheless did not consider the project would then be a military failure, it seems that the advocates of the use of plutonium fuel have much more exacting standards. Dr. Avery of BNFL suggests that a force equipped with such weapons would hardly be a "genuine nuclear force." I suppose this is a matter of definition. Dr. Avery's definition, however, is unlikely to be accepted by a country without nuclear weapons facing an adversary with such weapons. In 1945, the United States used only two nuclear weapons in the low kiloton range, and these were enough to bring quite a large war to conclusion.

Several other issues raised at the hearings require extended comment: the kinds of restriction needed on transfers of nuclear technology, if even an improved inspection is to recognize signals of a military program; the limits of the obligation imposed by Article IV of the Nonproliferation Treaty to transfer various nuclear technologies; and the kinds of costs and risks which might influence the decision to move toward nuclear weapons.

Military Signals and Civilian Noise

The problem presented by the spread to many countries of civilian stocks of highly enriched uranium or plutonium or facilities that could quickly produce these materials is that such stocks would carry these countries so far along the path that leads also to nuclear explosives that from the moment that their military purpose becomes unambiguous, the additional time to get nuclear explosives would be too short for any feasible inspection system to provide timely warning. And timely warning, it has long been recognized, is the most that a feasible international inspection system can provide. The IAEA has no police force. Moreover, one of the major factors affecting a government's decision to make a nuclear explosive will be not only the extra time from the point at which its military purpose becomes clear, but also the additional political risks and indeed the increment in resource costs above the costs expended for at least a plausibly pure civilian commercial activity.

Since the central aim of "effective safeguards" as explicitly defined in the IAEA information circulars on NPT safeguards is timely warning, signals of a military program must be detected and identified early enough; but they must also be unambiguous enough, that is, stand out clearly enough from the noisy background of civilian activity, to permit response either by international agencies, by regional allies, or by regional adversaries who have been relying on promises that the country observed will not acquire nuclear weapons. Programs and facilities overtly "dedicated" (to use the current jargon) to the purpose of getting bomb material present of course the least ambiguous signals. Some nuclear activities, facilities, and equipment that are regarded as having legitimately "civilian" applications may nonetheless advance a country significantly toward a military weapons capability. That is to say, they diminish the additional costs entailed by a decision to get the bomb. They reduce the remaining time it would take to get nuclear explosives, and they reduce also the additional political risks of exposure and counteraction. For usable warning time must be measured at best from the moment that indentification or differentiation from the noise is *reliably* made. For some sorts of response, the signals have to be not merely unambiguous enough, but they must also be public, i.e., usable without excessive risk of destroying sources.

Confusions of "Peaceful Use" with "Exclusively Peaceful Use"

The rhetoric of Atoms for Peace has tended, for countries aspiring to or undecided about whether to get nuclear weapons, to enhance the political utility of the ambiguity inherent in nominally civilian activities which in fact have a dual military and civilian character. With the one explicit exception of Plowshare (nuclear explosives for civil engineering), Article IV of the NPT is frequently interpreted as conferring legitimacy on all civilian activities, simply because they have some civilian function. This is so, even if they are not exclusively civilian in their import. As a result Article IV is often interpreted as obliging all advanced countries to transfer any civilian technology except Plowshare, no matter how far such transfer might carry the recipient country toward a military nuclear capability. Even some Agreements on Nuclear Cooperation between countries have been rather careless in failing to include or to stress the adverb "exclusively." And the trouble goes back to the beginning of the nuclear era, when we formed the habit of talking as if a civilian use automatically substituted for military utility, rather than some-times complementing or enhancing it.

However, the legislative history of the IAEA statute shows that "peaceful" was intended to mean "exclusively peaceful," as well it might in the common sense interpretation. In the United States, for example, the legislative history makes clear that U.S. senators have always been concerned that a civilian use should not also assist a country to get nuclear bombs. One illustration is the exchange be-tween Senator Sparkman and Secretary of State Dulles in the 1957 Hearings on the IAEA. The Senator asked, "Just what certainty is there that a particular peacetime project might not have a future military use as well as a peaceful one?" Secretary Dulles deferred to Chairman Strauss but gave his "untutored impression that since the material furnished will not itself be of weapon quality, and since the making, converting of it into weapon quality or the extraction of weapons quality material out of it as a byproduct would be an elab-orate and difficult and expensive operation, that could not occur without the knowledge of the agency and that the violation would be detected."[25] Senator Sparkman's concern addresses the plain com-mon sense meaning of Atoms for Peace and of the various Agree-ments on Nuclear Cooperation. In the same way, in reading the Non-proliferation Treaty we ought to keep in mind that the peaceful uses it wants to encourage are intended to be exclusively peaceful, not also military.

Now Article IV of the NPT refers to the undertaking by all parties to the treaty "to facilitate" and the right of all parties "to participate in, the fullest possible exchange of equipment, materials and scien-tific and technological information for the peaceful uses of nuclear energy." Indeed, it refers to such rights to the peaceful pursuit of nuclear energy, in the language of eighteenth-century natural law, as "inalienable." The contention was made by many of the delegates to the Iran Conference on Transfer of Nuclear Technology at Persepolis in the spring of 1977 that this "inalienable right" includes the stocking of plutonium or other highly concentrated fissile material and was therefore violated by President Carter's proposal to delay commitment to unrestricted commerce in plutonium. They made a declaration to that effect which has been characterized as a rebellion of the Third World countries against this violation of the NPT. This particular Third-World rebellion might have been a little more convincing if the president of the American Nuclear Society had not played a leading role in the writing of the declaration, and if some of the countries complaining most bitterly about a supposed violation of a most sacred part of the NPT had not themselves neglected ever to sign or ratify the NPT. However, Article IV explicitly states that the inalienable right of all parties to the treaty to the peaceful use of nuclear energy has to be in conformity with Articles I and II, and it is these articles that are what make the treaty a treaty against proliferation. In Article I the nuclear weapons states promise not to transfer or "in any way to assist, [or] encourage . . . any nonnuclear-weapons state to manufacture" nuclear explosives. If the fullest possible exchange were taken to include the provision of stocks of highly concentrated fissile material within days or hours of being ready for incorporation into an explosive, this would certainly "assist" an aspiring nonnuclear-weapons state in making such an explosive. No reasonable interpretation of the Nonproliferation Treaty would say that the treaty intends, in exchange for a quite revocable promise by countries without nuclear explosives not to make or acquire them, to transfer to them material that is within days or hours of being ready for incorporation in a bomb. Some help and certainly the avoidance of *arbitrary* interference in peaceful uses of nuclear energy are involved. However, the main return for promising not to manufacture or receive nuclear weapons is clearly a corresponding promise by some potential adversaries, backed by a system to provide early warning if the promises should be broken. The NPT is, after all, a treaty against proliferation, not for nuclear development.

Increase of Civilian Nuclear Noise Through Laxity in Project Economics

The practice of promoting and undertaking civilian nuclear activities which may confer prestige but have no strict economic justification has increased the noise background which serves as a potential cover for military activities. The IAEA has as part of its charter the mission of accelerating and enlarging the benefits of civilian uses of nuclear energy, with special regard for the developing countries. It is worth observing, however, that the principal international agency charged with financing international economic development, namely the International Bank for Reconstruction and Development, has, because it wants to support economic development rather than status or prestige, explicitly refused to finance any nuclear project in the less developed world, and not only the most dubious projects like small reprocessing plants, or the cumulation of fissile stocks likely to be idle for decades. Nuclear electric power is in general highly capital intensive, efficient only in very large sizes, and requires continuing highly sophisticated maintenance, characteristics which do not in general fit the needs of less developed countries. Expenditures for using plutonium fuel in breeders are in general even more inappropriate. However dubious the civilian value of some nuclear projects, their military applicability may be quite definite. The most familiar example is Plowshare, which has yet to demonstrate a realistic economic application, but which—because of the laxity of economic analysis applied to such projects—has served as a nominally civilian cover for an activity with obvious military implications. In this case the lack of rigor in the economic analysis, indeed the nearly total absence of any economic analysis at all, has reinforced the error involved in ignoring the point that "Atoms for Peace" means "exclusively for peace." These particular atoms for "peace" are in fact likely to be useful exclusively for war. Article V of the NPT therefore excludes "peaceful" nuclear explosives.

Plowshare, however, is merely the most familiar case. The careless way in which nuclear establishments in the mid-1950s and at the beginning of the 1960s decided to separate plutonium and to accumulate it for the distant and uncertain date at which it might be used for the initial load of a breeder reactor, ignored any rigorous economic criterion for investments over time. A rigorous criterion would maximize the productive use of current resources and so increase the resources available for future generations. When India decided in the mid-1950s to invest in a separation facility and in stocks of plutonium which in essence would be economically idle for many decades—until the hoped-for appearance of a thorium breeder, or near-breeder—this was a waste of capital in a developing country where capital is particularly scarce. Yet the activity served to increase the noise level and the opportunities and ease for a decision to make military nuclear explosives, when circumstances changed.

Plowshare has for a long time been a rather transparent cover for a military purpose. However, it seems that decisions to stock separated plutonium for the breeder began as sincerely but badly conceived economic measures. Many other countries besides India, including Japan, decided very early to accumulate plutonium, not for recycle in light-water reactors, but for the breeder. These early decisions were made with little economic analysis, on the basis of quite unrealistic anticipations of the uncertain dates at which breeders might be of commercial importance. In India, however, these early decisions made on other grounds served to prepare for a program of nuclear explosives. More recent decisions to acquire either stocks of plutonium separated elsewhere, or a national separation plant, are likely to be from the outset more self-consciously related to military plans. For example, Pakistan, which has no reactors requiring fuel enriched by either uranium or plutonium, sometimes insists that the separation plant it is purchasing from France is purely civilian in intent, and on the other hand sometimes says that it will be glad to give up plutonium separation, provided that the superpowers abandon their own nuclear weapons. (See, for example, *Dawn Overseas*, Islamabad, June 19, 1977: "Mr. Bhutto said Pakistan was ready to cancel its deal with France if the Nuclear Powers gave a solemn pledge to destroy each and every nuclear weapon.") Which rather directly, if consistently, acknowledges that Pakistan's purpose in separating plutonium is only to make nuclear weapons to balance those of "Nuclear Powers" and that this purpose would be served equally by the destruction of everybody else's nuclear weapons.

Incremental Definitions of Critical Cost, Time, and Risks in the Decision to Obtain Explosive Material

Opponents of any delay in commitment to commerce in plutonium argue that restrictions on such commerce, for example by prohibiting reprocessing plants or MOX fabrication plants (or presumably also stocks of plutonium dioxide or mixed oxide) under national controls, cannot prevent a country "determined" to arm itself with nuclear weapons from doing so. Such a determined country could always choose either to make highly enriched uranium (which is admittedly difficult today and restricted to very few countries), or (what is much easier and more direct) to make plutonium in a simple production reactor and separate it in a small scale reprocessing plant.[26] These arguments, which suggest that any country that wants to can easily get material ready for use in a nuclear explosive, are inconsistent with the associated affirmation that it would be very useful to improve safeguards without restricting technology. They have, however, other technical and conceptual flaws.

According to the late Harry Johnson[27] of the London School of Economics and the University of Chicago, who spent much of the 1960s on OECD and on U.K. and U.S. government committees examining French, British, and American science policy, one major trouble stemmed from the limitations of natural scientists and technologists as advisors on science policy. He mentions specifically limitations in understanding the concept of measuring benefits, compared with costs "at the margin" of an activity—as economists would put it. Whether or not this conceptual limitation troubles science policy in general, it does plague many recent attempts to compare the "proliferation resistance" of alternative fuel cycles. In particular it plagues the oddly self-defeating attempts by advocates of plutonium fuel to demonstrate that all fuel cycles are equally dangerous, or to show that facilities dedicated exclusively to the production and separation of plutonium are even cheaper and better ways of getting a nuclear bomb "for a nation determined to get one," than the use of plutonium from civilian power reactors and civilian separation plants.

A civilian power reactor of the size now being sold might cost a billion dollars, and rather more in a less developed country. A separation facility capable of handling one or two hundred metric tons of spent uranium oxide fuel per year might cost one or two hundred million dollars, judging from the recent Japanese experience at Tokai Mura. A 1,500-ton per year separation plant including conversion from nitrate to oxide, might cost over a billion dollars, and these facilities might take ten years or so to build.

On the other hand, estimates of the cost of facilities "dedicated" to producing and separating plutonium for a few weapons per year will vary among other things according to the degree of optimism of the estimator about the corners a country might cut in neglecting considerations of safety, the amount of help it receives from outside, the continued availability without restraint of some of the needed components, and the efficiency of the particular small or less developed country. (The myth present in some of these estimates has persisted since the early 1950s: that because construction labor is cheaper in developing countries, costs will be lower. A good deal of evidence has been accumulating since that time, that the costs will in general be much higher, even with extensive outside technical help[28]). In any case, the costs of "dedicated" facilities are generally estimated in the tens or hundreds of millions rather than in billions.

To be sure one should not take such cost estimates entirely seriously, as one of the estimators himself notes.[29] Even in the United States, on the basis of long experience and the highest available expertise, much more detailed and elaborate estimates greatly understate the costs of various reprocessing facilities. For example, General Electric was off by a factor of nearly 400 percent from its initial estimate of $17 million for its Morris, Illinois plant at the point when it abandoned the plant. According to Lamarsh, it would take another $120 million to put it in order. As for the AGNS plant, Lamarsh says it has cost over $200 million compared to the initial $70 million estimate, and might take another $400 million to meet all requirements. Nonetheless, if one considers total rather than marginal or incremental costs, it would seem plausible to suppose that "dedicated" facilities cost at least an order of magnitude less than civilian power and separation facilities presently being sold.

But to consider total rather than incremental costs misses the main point, which is that decisions should be considered at the margin, that it is the *extra* costs incurred by the decision to acquire nuclear weapons which count in making the decision. For in making a decision to build a reactor exclusively dedicated to plutonium production for weapons and to build a reprocessing plant exclusively for the purpose of separating such material, all of the costs of such facilities are the result of the decision to obtain weapons material.

On the other hand, if one has already acquired a nuclear reactor with an overtly civilian use, and has also acquired either a separation facility, or the separation services of another country, or stocks of plutonium from any source, or stocks of mixed oxide fuel directly under one's own control, or possibly even stocks of plutonium or highly enriched uranium metal for civilian critical experiments, then the decision to use these facilities or stocks can yield explosive material with very little extra effort and only trivial costs.

Depending on which of these civilian starting points we assume, the incremental costs might be in millions of dollars, or in the case of critical experiments as low as thousands or tens of thousands of dollars, to get the highly concentrated fissile material ready for incorporation in a bomb. So the relevant cost comparison in incremental terms would suggest that the civilian route to bomb material may proceed along a legitimate path for so much of the way that the cost of proceeding down the final military branch is anywhere from one to five orders of magnitude lower than the route by way of totally dedicated facilities—*not*, as one might infer if one considered total rather than incremental costs, one or two orders of magnitude higher.

Similar things can be said about the total and incremental time (as distinct from cost) to get nuclear material for weapons. And this is crucial in judging the political risks for the country getting the weapons as well as in determining the opportunities for response by the international community or by specific countries whose interests are affected. If a country follows the course sometimes claimed to be not only the most direct, but the easiest, and sets out overtly to dedicate facilities to the production and separation of plutonium, the incremental time that is relevant starts at the outset. On Lamarsh's estimate, for example, that time might last about six years: four years for a small or developing country to build a plant modeled on the Brookhaven graphite research reactor, capable of yielding annually spent fuel containing one or two bombs' worth of plutonium; another year to get that amount of spent fuel, and then if the separation facility has been built in parallel, another period of time, depending mainly on the cooling period, the throughput, and the risks undertaken to do the actual separation and conversion to oxide powder or metal. (It is worth noting that the clandestine construction and operation of such a reactor is likely to be easily detectable by many means including sensors in satellites. It is a large construction enterprise and the operation of nuclear production reactors would yield very large thermal and other signatures.)

The point of a civilian cover is to reduce the interval between what is overtly civilian and what is unambiguously military. In the cases discussed above, where stocks of mixed oxide fuel or separated plutonium under national control have an accepted civilian use, according to the prevailing convention, the incremental time might be measured in weeks or days. If plutonium and highly enriched uranium metal stocks are legitimate, it would be a matter of days or hours.

The ten years or so that might be involved in acquiring these civilian power and separation facilities are not relevant, then, in determining the risks of undertaking an overt or obvious military program. Those ten years or so are indeed longer than the five or six years to traverse the direct path through overt dedicated facilities. But the path that maintains the maximum civilian cover before breaking out openly would have an exposed final military portion smaller by two to four orders of magnitude than the direct overt path.

The incremental times and costs that are relevant depend on an enforceable or observed convention as to when an activity ceases to be exclusively or legitimately civilian. Advocates of the use of plutonium fuel in civilian power reactors argue that production reactors that are dedicated to the purpose of getting weapons and reprocessing plants that are specifically designed and devoted to separating the spent fuel from these reactors for weapons grade material are a cheaper and better route. Insofar as these are overtly dedicated, these advocates are clearly wrong. The relevant costs, times, and risks all then stem from the overt military purpose. Of course just as a power reactor which might be really intended to supply weapons material can serve as a cover for a military purpose, there are covers for production reactors too. Specifically they may be called research reactors. But large production reactors that are nominally for research are no longer likely to be taken at face value. At any rate the principal object of the new conventions about export sales should be to prevent the use of such a cover, to find adequate substitutes for any genuine civilian purpose, such as training facilities elsewhere, etc.

Similarly, separation facilities were once accepted as normal concomitants of the civilian fuel cycle of the future. The object of the Ford-Carter program is to alter that convention. Then the incremental time and incremental cost can be said to start at the point at which the new convention is breached, from the moment when the military purpose becomes overt or at least obvious enough for response.

WHAT MIGHT MAKE A COUNTRY "DETERMINED" TO GET NUCLEAR WEAPONS?

Those who are for an immediate commitment to commerce in plutonium are in the habit of starting their assertions with phrases like "A
nation that makes the political decision to arm itself with nuclear
weapons can always, etc."; or "Countries determined to get nuclear
weapons will, etc." But such assertions evade the main issue, which is
to discourage countries from becoming so "determined."

A policy to prevent or slow the spread of nuclear weapons must
consider factors infuencing a country to change its mind when it is
undecided or has even definitely decided against acquiring nuclear
weapons. Such factors, as I have indicated, are complex. They include among other things the threats a country might perceive and
its alternatives for meeting these threats without nuclear weapons.
But they surely include also the additional costs and risks that would
be incurred by the decision and the period of time during which the
country in question would be exposed to the risk of counteraction.
This period of exposure and the political military risks in general
plainly depend on the interval of time during which a movement toward getting nuclear explosive material is clearly distinguishable from
what is accepted as legitimate civilian nuclear activity.

*Since inspection systems are directed at detecting illegitimate
actions, inspection alone cannot substitute for a redefinition of conventions of legitimacy.* Present conventions allow activities to come
too close to a bomb to give a warning system time to work. Control
of stocks of highly enriched uranium or plutonium makes it easier
for a country to change its mind, when political circumstances
change, and to decide then to get nuclear weapons. It is also easier
for a government to make such decisions one step at a time rather
than all at once.

A paper cited by BNFL as authority for the irrelevance of a ban
on the transfer of sensitive technologies because "it would not
prevent states from developing nuclear weapons once they had decided to do so," immediately admits that a ban "would, however,
slow the progress of a weapons programme and might also have an
influence on the decision process itself."[30] That admission, damaging
enough, puts the matter much too mildly.

When a country is moving toward a nuclear capability under the
cover of legitimate activities, it may receive not only cooperation but
subsidies from states with nuclear weapons. But if it should be seen
unambiguously to be undertaking an illegitimate action directed at a
military nuclear program, it is unlikely to receive such help and may
be exposed to great peril. For that reason, even thin disguises have

The line between supplier countries and importing countries is already blurred and shifting; it will tend to lose significance in time. There are also practical problems. If, for example, uranium from Canada is converted to enrichment plant feed in Britain, enriched in the United States, and fabricated in Germany, the resulting fuel may be subject to several layers of overlapping and probably diverse bilateral controls. This leads to a cat's cradle of administrative controls. Even if there are no overlapping controls, some suppliers may be more permissive than others. We clearly need a set of universally accepted standards for nuclear commerce. There is an embryonic start on this in the nuclear suppliers conference, but this expedient is only a stopgap.

I would like to propose a scheme for internationalizing reprocessing control. The necessary control provisions would be satisfied for each exporter by approval of a model agreement between the recipient and a suitable international body—perhaps an entirely new institution—embodying an undertaking not to reprocess nuclear fuel until this is permitted by the international body, rather than by any individual supplier, or any group of suppliers.

Under this scheme no reprocessing at all would be allowed to take place until the international organization makes a general finding that the world community can cope with the associated risks of proliferation—perhaps a future finding that as a consequence of the introduction of technological and institutional innovation "reprocessing can now take place without increasing the risks of proliferation beyond that of the once-through fuel cycle."

It would not be altogether novel for the United States to turn over reprocessing controls to an appropriate international entity, for it is analogous to our assignment of bilateral inspection rights to the IAEA in the 1960s. Similarly, reprocessing control provisions in our Agreements for Cooperation could provide for transfer to an international entity when it is ready and able to carry out this function. Such a transfer should be contingent on a congressional finding that "effective and enforceable international reprocessing controls are available."

The often heard criticism that the United States is trying to impose its will on trading partners can best be answered by our agreement to be bound by the same rules and the same international discipline as others. If all countries participate in the reprocessing findings, fears that the United States is trying to impose a double standard can be allayed. Such a scheme would extend and reinforce the element of restraint represented by the president's deferral of U.S. commercial reprocessing and restructuring of its breeder programs, both of which have been met with skepticism abroad.

CONCLUSION

What are the chances for President Carter's new nuclear energy policies to gain acceptance? I am obliged to say that there are dishearteningly few, inside or outside the government, who are convinced that the United States can make a difference, and who are there to plead the president's case against nuclear proliferation.

The counsels of nuclear appeasement are many. The president, they say, is overreacting to a problem of no great proportions; or, the problem is too big for the United States to undertake alone, and none will follow our lead; or, it is too late—plutonium is inevitable, proliferation is inevitable; or our example counts for little, others will continue their plans for reprocessing no matter what we do.

But there are also signs that others abroad are listening. What is needed now is time—time to reflect on the proliferation problem, on the nuclear energy alternatives, and on the need for stricter international discipline in the uses of nuclear energy. The president's decision to pause in the separation and use of plutonium is designed to buy that time.

For thirty years and throughout the administrations of six presidents it has been a cardinal principle of U.S. nuclear policy that at least none of our materials or equipment finds its way into the nuclear weapons of nations not already in possession of them.

Yet we now know that American heavy water played a role in producing the plutonium used in the 1974 Indian nuclear explosion. Unless that lesson is taken to heart we are going to see it happen again.

And next time it will be a greal deal harder to explain to our children.

NOTE TO CHAPTER 4

1. *Nucleonics Week*, "Carter Policy Seems Damaging to U.S. Non-proliferation Credibility," Vol. 18, No. 15, April 14, 1977, pp. 1–2.

✳ *Chapter 5*

Nuclear Energy
and the Proliferation
of Nuclear Weapons

Victor Gilinsky

In this discussion, prepared just over three months after the California Seminar talk comprising Chapter 4, Commissioner Gilinsky reviews the history of nuclear energy policy and gives some technical reasons why current international safeguards are inadequate if fuel cycles involving reprocessing are used. He concludes with a plea for a better common understanding of what is dangerous and what is not. The talk, which was given at the Washington Center of Foreign Policy Research, Johns Hopkins University, on November 3, 1977, refers to a bill, then pending in the Congress, to tighten safeguards on the export of nuclear material, equipment, and technology to prevent their use in development of nuclear weapons. This legislation, the Nuclear Nonproliferation Act of 1978, was signed into law on March 10, 1978, and gives Congress the right to review and veto Executive Branch policies on nuclear nonproliferation. (It is not without interest that the first nuclear export license to be reviewed by the Nuclear Regulatory Commission under this new law concerned the shipment of nuclear fuels to the Government of India. The commission was unable to agree on issuance of the license and the application was forwarded to the president, who subsequently authorized it.)

It is still too early to tell how implementation of the new law will affect the further spread of nuclear weapons. Much will depend on whether the need for more thoughtful policies in the future suggested in this discussion is recognized. For this reason it is an apt conclusion for our collection.

The relationship between nuclear electric power and nuclear weapons development is central to any policy on the use of nuclear energy internationally as well as domestically. As our understanding of it has changed over the years, so has our policy.

The most recent metamorphosis has taken place in consequence of the seriousness with which President Carter has viewed the peaceful-military connection in nuclear energy. In a major statement on nuclear policy on April 7, 1977, and again on October 19 in remarks to the organizing session of the forty-nation International Nuclear Fuel Cycle Evaluation Conference, he outlined a clear change in attitude and direction toward civilian nuclear power and its role in increasing the danger that nuclear weapons will spread to more and more countries. This matter is also addressed in a bill, the Nuclear Nonproliferation Act of 1977,[a] now before the Congress. It seeks to impose stricter rules on U.S. nuclear exports to make sure they do not get used for explosives.

The bill has passed the House of Representatives by a vote of 411 to 0, but encountered heavy weather in the Senate this session, partly because of intense lobbying by some elements of the nuclear industry. Their position, in practical effect, has been that the relationship between the commercial nuclear fuel cycle and nuclear explosives is so remote that further controls are unnecessary—or, alternatively, if not remote, then so far gone that it is too late to reverse. On each side of the issues underlying a recommended nuclear export policy is a conception of the relationship between nuclear energy and nuclear proliferation. As the president said on October 19, the subject is inherently controversial and can stand some clarification.

ACCESS TO NUCLEAR EXPLOSIVE MATERIALS

I do not want to dwell here on technical details, but a few remarks may be helpful. The essential nuclear explosive ingredients of nuclear warheads are plutonium or highly enriched uranium. You may recall that plutonium for our own nuclear weapons program has been produced in large special-purpose reactors and separated from the spent fuel in reprocessing plants at Hanford, Washington and Savannah River, Georgia. The highly enriched uranium has come from a complex of plants at Oak Ridge, Tennessee and similar facilities in Kentucky and Ohio, all of which are now used primarily to enrich uranium fuel for power reactors throughout the world.

The generation of electricity by nuclear means raises international security issues because uranium-fueled nuclear power reactors also produce plutonium. Commercial spent fuel reprocessing plants, which separate plutonium, provide easy physical access to large quantities of nuclear explosive material. And the same technologies (and in some cases the same plants) are used to enrich it further for explosive purposes.

The essential point is this: obtaining the requisite explosive

---

[a]Later changed to the Nuclear Nonproliferation Act of 1978.

material is still the most difficult and time-consuming item in the initial production of nuclear weapons.[1] The operation of civilian nuclear power reactors and certain ancillary facilities—plutonium separation and uranium enrichment plants—can therefore remove key technological hurdles in this process and make it easier for a country to manufacture nuclear warheads, and quickly, once it decides to do so.

Such a decision will, of course, depend on the political and military situation in which a country finds itself at the moment of truth. Still, any serious antiproliferation policy, in addition to reducing the incentives to acquire nuclear weapons that grow out of genuine security concerns, must also aim at keeping it from being technically too easy to take up the military option. It is this latter question I wish to address.

The degree to which physical access to the essential nuclear explosive ingredients of nuclear warheads—either plutonium or highly enriched uranium—is facilitated by the operation of the commercial nuclear fuel cycle depends on the kinds and sizes of nuclear facilities in place and how the fuel cycle is operated. The important distinction between less dangerous and more dangerous fuel cycle activities forms the basis of current U.S. policy—which supports the relatively safe activities and seeks to restrict the dangerous. The line that is drawn between the two is not popular, either with the uncompromising opponents of nuclear energy (who regard all its aspects as equally dangerous), or with its zealous supporters (who until now have resisted labeling any aspect of the fuel cycle as dangerous).

SOME HISTORICAL PERSPECTIVE

Some historical perspective on this distinction is useful. U.S. nuclear energy policy was from the first based on a keen awareness of the dangerous aspect of nuclear electric power. The Acheson-Lilienthal Report of 1946 (which makes pretty good reading thirty years later) concluded that the only safe way to exploit nuclear power was under international supervision and control. The report recommended that dangerous elements in the nuclear fuel cycle—those that provided direct access to nuclear explosive materials—be placed under international ownership, but the related U.S. proposal to the United Nations was not adopted, in part because the Soviet Union would not agree to participate. (It is interesting to speculate on what might have happened had we gone forward without the Russians.) What did happen was that by the mid-fifties individual countries were proceeding to develop their own nuclear programs, encouraged and assisted by the U.S. Atoms for Peace program.

An International Atomic Energy Agency was established in 1957, primarily to monitor the flow of commercial nuclear materials and equipment among member countries wishing to avail themselves of these services. Although the fact that nuclear explosive materials were dangerous and should be kept out of harm's way was recognized—Article XII of the agency's 1957 charter speaks of IAEA custody over "excess" quantities of plutonium as a means of avoiding their accumulation in individual states—the use of plutonium and highly enriched uranium was not specifically restricted beyond requirements for agency inspections.

The security implications of a course that led to easy access to nuclear explosive material in national stockpiles were apparently not obvious to the nuclear policymakers of the fifties and the sixties. The prospect of many nations in possession of substantial quantities of nuclear explosive materials all seemed very far away; nuclear weapons were assumed to be enormously difficult to design and fabricate; and the U.S. near monopoly on the technology, fuels, and equipment for civilian nuclear power activities worldwide seemed to ensure U.S. control of the situation. Fledgling nuclear power programs were not thought then to have much to do with the development of nuclear weapons. The earlier prescience of the Acheson-Lilienthal group that they had everything to do with it was ignored. It is paradoxical that the true believers in technological progress did not contemplate the logical extension of that progress.

This may be explained in part by the fact that there was some genuine confusion on the technical side. It was once widely thought, for example, that "reactor grade" plutonium—that typically derived from spent power reactor fuel—was not suitable for use in nuclear weapons. This misconception about the possibility of "denaturing" plutonium, which seems to have originated in the Acheson-Lilienthal Report, persisted until recently in many quarters—a confusion which apparently even the IAEA shared.

The unfortunate result was that many of those responsible for protection against diversion of plutonium to military uses were working under the impression that technological barriers against misuse of plutonium made their job of protecting the public easier. In fact, those technological barriers did not exist.

A CHANGE IN CIRCUMSTANCES

The situation is now altered and there is no longer any innocent excuse for the perpetuation of the notion that reactor-grade plutonium cannot be used for weapons. The U.S. government has stated unambiguously that this material can be used to produce militarily important nuclear weapons, and that a device using reactor grade plutonium has been successfully tested. The fact is that in simple designs for nuclear weapons plutonium from power reactors can be used to produce explosions with yields reliably in the range of kilotons—by any conventional measure highly powerful explosions. I stress this last point because some of those who argued it could not be done have fallen back to discounting the military significance of explosions of this size.

Information gaps have also been closed in the current version of the IAEA Safeguards Technical Manual, which provides the following guidance: plutonium of any grade, in either metal, oxide, or nitrate form can be put in a form suitable for the manufacture of nuclear explosive devices in a matter of days to weeks.

To make full use of such a technical possibility, a country would have to perform the necessary preparatory work in advance, and secretly. This is a threat, however, that has now taken on a reality not present when the basic international rules for nuclear trade were formulated twenty years ago.

There have been other changes that contribute to the immediacy of the proliferation danger posed by commercial activities. First, the civilian nuclear power industry has grown enormously and by any reasonable measure (the plutonium production rate or the size of uranium enrichment facilities being utilized) exceeds the scale of the world's military nuclear programs. In fact, in most countries the quantities of plutonium in spent reactor fuel, if separated out and stored, will dwarf any plausible military needs.

At the same time technical possibilities expand, however, the political alternatives for a country seeking nuclear weapons are narrowing. There is no question that as the dangers of proliferation gradually sink in, the major nuclear exporters are showing less inclination to continue the laissez-faire approach that has unfortunately characterized nuclear trade in recent years. The time is fast approaching when a country can no longer count on the international community to look the other way while it openly puts together an explosives program, even if it does so without violating the strict letter of various international cooperative agreements.

The recent alarm over the possibility of a nuclear test in South Africa and the international attempt to intercept it underlines this point. Ironically, it also emphasizes to any would-be nuclear weapons state the critical importance of concealing its intentions up until the last moment before an explosion.

A NEW POLICY FOR A NEW SITUATION

These considerations reflect a fundamental change in the nuclear state of affairs internationally. It is a change that forces us to confront the inescapable fact that parts of the civilian and military aspects of nuclear energy are too closely related for comfort. Once that fact is accepted, a change in nuclear policy is mandatory. The Acheson-Lilienthal group saw the dangers clearly; their view led to the decision, in 1946, to try to internationalize atomic energy. When that failed, the United States withdrew into a period of secrecy. Eventually we became more relaxed about the development of nuclear energy for peaceful purposes and secrecy was abandoned. Because we mistakenly thought that civilian reactor safeguards could be stretched to cover the more dangerous elements in the fuel cycle—such as plutonium reprocessing when that day came—we allowed plans for the use of plutonium to go forward unhampered. There is where the damage was done.

The increased size and worldwide growth of the nuclear industry, the prospective availability of plutonium, and the inability to safeguard plutonium properly against the possibility that it would be used for weapons as well as fuel led to a reassessment of the dangers; at the same time, the sharply increased projected costs of commercial reprocessing led to a critical reevaluation of the economic advantages of an early commitment to plutonium use. This in turn led to the shift in nuclear policy reflected in the actions of Presidents Ford and Carter in their efforts to restrict access to dangerous materials, to pause in the commitment to plutonium separation and use, and to search for alternatives to national stockpiling. In a sense we are now doing what we failed to do twenty years ago—thinking ahead.

Unfortunately it is getting a little late; our domestic industry and our international trading partners perceive the shift in nuclear policy as a threat to nuclear power, and they are pulling very hard in the opposite direction. The controversy is intense, and every conceivable argument against making any connection between civilian and military uses of nuclear energy has been put forward.

WHAT ABOUT UNSAFEGUARDED
PRODUCTION REACTORS?

It is contended, for example, that no country choosing to build nuclear weapons would turn to its civilian power reactors for the requisite explosive materials. To divert material in this way would risk detection by the IAEA inspectors and in addition would provide too poor a grade of plutonium to interest weaponeers. Under this self-serving theory, if weapons material is wanted, a special-purpose, unsafeguarded reactor would be built. It is possible at the moment to do this legally in countries not party to the Nonproliferation Treaty and therefore not subject to inspection of *all* its indigenous nuclear facilities. This underlines the need to extend the requirements of the treaty to nonsignatory nations by conditioning nuclear trade on acceptance of international agreements and inspection on *all* nuclear activities within importing countries. There is increasing pressure to do this, and the bill now before the Congress makes this a condition for U.S. nuclear exports.

Even if legal, however, the construction of a special-purpose plutonium production reactor signals a country's intention to build bombs and, in the present climate, risks premature interception of its attempt to obtain explosive material for nuclear weapons. This risk can be avoided, however, by stockpiling separated plutonium from spent power plant fuel openly and legally. A defense establishment can design and fabricate a bomb in privacy; the illegal activity is then confined to a swift, almost one-step process: appropriation from its storage place of the necessary plutonium, fabrication, and insertion into the waiting bomb. It is surely the quickest, cheapest, and least risky route to nuclear weapons. So long as individual nations are permitted to keep nuclear explosive stockpiles they are, in effect, in possession of an option to make nuclear weapons almost literally overnight.

CAN WE RELY ON INTERNATIONAL SAFEGUARDS?

But, it is argued, if these nuclear activities are placed under the protection of international safeguards, it is not necessary to put constraints on plutonium reprocessing or uranium enrichment. All that is needed is to beef up the IAEA's current inspections—more inspectors, more equipment. But safeguarding reactors and their fuel— typically many technological steps from use for nuclear weapons— is one thing; "safeguarding" the nuclear explosive material itself is quite another.

Periodic inspections of nuclear power programs involving only power reactors can provide a significant degree of protection by providing international warning of possible wrongdoing. This is because it takes many months or years to obtain the plutonium separation capability to turn reactor fuel into a form usable for weapons; awareness of a reliable advance warning system that would spot such activity serves as a deterrent to illicit bomb programs. It is important here to appreciate the vital element of time: the object of international inspection is to frustrate the purpose of the diversion by ringing an alarm *in time* to allow for counteraction by the international community. If sufficient time for effective response is not provided, "safeguards" will not work.

In other words, from the moment spent reactor fuel is translated into separated plutonium and stored, the element of "timely" warning, on which our present safeguards system has been relying, evaporates. The same is true, of course, for stockpiles of highly enriched uranium.

It is important to understand that so far as safeguards are concerned, a stock of nuclear explosive material is a great deal more like a bomb than it is like a reactor. No one would dream of suggesting that nuclear explosive devices, regardless of how labeled, should be exported under international safeguards. The Nonproliferation Treaty settled once and for all the notion that nuclear explosives came in two categories, military and peaceful. Under the treaty no such distinction is permitted. Yet strip away the electronics and the conventional high explosives and label the plutonium as intended for peaceful purposes and many nuclear spokesmen, at home and abroad, will tell you that if subject to occasional inspections it is a perfectly safe proposition: just like safeguarding power reactors.

AGREEING ON COMMON RULES

Two U.S. presidents have decided otherwise. They perceived a serious safeguards deficiency and moved to change U.S. policy in consequence. The primary imperative of the new policy is to develop common rules for international nuclear trade. But before these rules can be formulated, much less implemented, it will be necessary to arrive at a common understanding of what is dangerous and what is not. It is clear that such an understanding does not yet exist, as witness export sales by our nuclear trading partners of plutonium reprocessing and uranium enrichment facilities. Common understanding must extend as well to how much the spread of nuclear weapons threatens individual countries and world security. This is a tricky matter, because intense international competition in nuclear commerce is involved—with its accompanying heavy investment as well as national pride—and tends to obscure the threat.

The fear of additional controls and their impact on international markets has led our own nuclear industry to attack the validity of the distinction being drawn between nuclear reactors and their low-enriched uranium fuel (a comparatively benign combination when subject to comprehensive oversight) and the more dangerous situation in which individual countries have access to facilities for the separation and storage of the plutonium derived from the operation of their power reactors. In the face of all evidence to the contrary, they have steadfastly insisted that international inspections of plutonium reprocessing activities will adequately protect against the danger of proliferation.

Their argument has now taken an odd turn. The lobbyists against control legislation maintain that the restrictions on commercial reprocessing facilities proposed by the president and the Congress involve a sacrifice without reward—no added safety can derive from such an action. According to industry spokesmen, just as countries with legal access to plutonium might design and fabricate weapons secretly, so countries without such legal access might also, without much added effort, reprocess spent fuel secretly in a small clandestine facility. I happen to think that one is relatively easy to hide and the other more difficult and risky (certainly doing both is more risky), and that the government's effort to make a distinction between the two cases is valid. What is most interesting, however, is that this latest wrinkle in the effort to forestall implementation of the new policy has led to some strange bedfellows. By saying, in effect, that all forms of nuclear power are equally dangerous, the nuclear industry seems to be agreeing with its most uncompromising opponents that the situation is far worse than the rest of us thought. Where that will take us is something I will leave to more fertile imaginations.

NOTE TO CHAPTER 5

1. See the 1975 Encyclopedia Americana article on Nuclear Weapons by John Foster, previously the Defense Department's R & D chief and a former director of the Livermore Laboratory: "It must be appreciated that the only difficult part of making a fission bomb of some sort is the preparation of a supply of fissionable material of adequate purity; the design of the bomb itself is relatively easy." *Encyclopedia Americana*, Vol. 20 (New York: Americana Corporation, 1975), pp. 518-528.

California Seminar
on Arms Control
and Foreign Policy

SELECTED REPORTS OF THE
CALIFORNIA SEMINAR

ADDITIONAL SEMINAR PUBLICATIONS

Number 21   Johnson, William A. *U.S. Military Aid Programs and Conventional Arms Control.* January 1973. ($1.25)

   22   Canby, Steven L. *NATO Muscle: More Shadow than Substance.* February 1973. ($1.25)

   23   Gurtov, Melvin. *Secession and Intervention: U.S. Policy in the Congo and Bangladesh.* March 1973. ($1.25)

   24   Kerr, Malcolm. *American Policy Toward Egypt, 1955-1971: A Record of Failures.* March 1973 ($1.25)

   25   Packenham, Robert A. *The United States and Third World Development.* March 1973. ($1.25)

   26   Cohen, Samuel T. *SALT and the Test Ban: Parallels and Prospects.* May 1973. ($1.25)

   27   Schwartz, Morton. *The Failed Symbiosis: The USSR and Leftist Regimes in Less Developed Countries.* May 1973. ($1.25)

   28   Serfaty, Simon. *America and Europe in the Seventies: Integration or Disintegration?* May 1973. (Out of print)

   29   Serfaty, Simon. *The International Anomaly: America, France and the French Communist Party, 1945-1947.* May 1973. ($1.25)

   30   York, Herbert F. *SALT I and the Future of Arms Control and Disarmament.* May 1973. ($1.25)

   31   Serfaty, Simon. *No More Dissent?* July 1973. (Out of print)

   32   Edwards, Catherine. *U.S. Policy and the Japanese Nuclear Option.* August 1973. ($1.25)

   33   Halle, Louis J. *The Question of Commitment.* September 1973. ($1.25)

   34   Spiegel, Steven L. *The Patron Meets the Pygmies: U.S. Trials in the Arab-Israeli Theater.* September 1973. ($1.25)

   36   Einaudi, Luigi. *Peru and Chile: What Do They Imply for the United States?* January 1974. ($1.25)

   37   Elliot, David C. *The United Kingdom and Arms Control, 1963-1973.* January 1974. ($1.25)

   38   Jenkins, Brian, Cesar Sereseres, and Luigi Einaudi. *U.S. Military Aid and Guatemalan Politics.* March 1974. ($1.25)

   39   Baker, Steven. *Italy and the Nuclear Option.* May 1974. ($1.25)

   40   Mendershausen, Horst. *Inoffensive Deterrence.* May 1974. ($1.25)

   41   Wohlstetter, Albert. *Threats and Promises of Peace: Europe and America in the New Era.* May 1974. (No charge—Reprint from *Orbis*, Winter 1974)

   42   Canby, Steven L. *Damping Nuclear Counterforce Incentives: Correcting NATO's Inferiority in Conventional Military Strength.* August 1974. ($1.25)

   43   Gilinsky, Victor. *Fueling the Western World's Reactors: Problems and Issues.* September 1974. (Out of print)

   45   Wohlstetter, Roberta. *International Terrorism: Kidnapping to Win Friends and Influence People.* September 1974. (No charge—Reprint from *Survey*, Autumn 1974)

46 Ball, Desmond. *Déjà Vu: The Return to Counterforce in the Nixon Administration.* December 1974. ($1.25)

47 Zoppo, Ciro. *The Nuclear Genie in the Mideast.* December 1974. (No charge—Reprint from *New Outlook*, February 1975)

48 Jenkins, Brian. *International Terrorism: A New Mode of Conflict.* January 1975. ($2.25—Available only from Crescent Publications, 5410 Wilshire Boulevard, Los Angeles, CA 90036)

49 Cooper, Charles. *The Challenge to the International Market Economy.* July 1975. ($1.25)

50 Langer, Paul and Richard Moorsteen. *The U.S.-Japanese Military Alliance: Japanese Perceptions and the Prospective Impact of Evolving U.S. Military Doctrines and Technologies.* February 1975. ($1.50)

51 Momoi, Makoto. *The Future of U.S.-Japanese Relations.* July 1975. ($1.50)

53 Zoppo, Ciro. *Trends in Nuclear Proliferation and U.S. Security.* July 1975. ($1.50)

55 Conine, Ernest. *Credits for the Soviet Union: Good Business or Foreign Aid to the Wealthy?* July 1975. ($2.25)

56 Brodie, Bernard. *How Much is Enough? Guns Versus Butter Revisited.* August 1975. ($1.25)

57 Zoppo, Ciro. *Naval Arms Control in the Mediterranean.* August 1975. ($2.25)

58 Barton, John. *A Free Market in Peaceful Nuclear Technology.* August 1975. ($1.50)

59 Holliday, Dennis and Vincent Taylor. *The Uncertain Future of Nuclear Power.* August 1975. ($1.50)

60 Kosaka, Masataka. *Detente and East Asia.* September 1975. ($1.50)

61 Nishihara, Masashi. *Agenda for Japan-U.S. Coordination in Southeast Asia.* September 1975. ($1.50)

62 Weinstein, Martin. *The U.S.-Japanese Alliance: Is There an Equivalent for Mutual Indispensability?* September 1975. ($1.50)

64 Jenkins, Brian. *Will Terrorists Go Nuclear?* October 1975. ($1.50)

65 Kobayashi, Katsumi. *The Nixon Doctrine and U.S.-Japanese Security Relations.* October 1975. ($1.50)

66 Gati, Tob Trister. *Soviet Perspectives on Nuclear Nonproliferation.* November 1975. ($1.50)

67 Harris, William R. *Safeguard Initiatives Under Conditions of Limited Nuclear Proliferation.* November 1975. ($1.50)

68 Luttwak, Edward. *U.S. Policy in a Proliferating World.* November 1975. ($1.50)

69 Palfrey, John. *U.S. Nonproliferation Strategy and the Transfer of Nuclear Technology.* November 1975. ($1.50)

70 Hoag, Malcolm. *U.S. Economic and Security Problems: Why Not Project Interdependence?* November 1975. ($2.25)

71 Hoffman, Fred. *Energy Use in Japan and United States: Questions and Policy Issues.* December 1975. ($1.50)

72 Caldwell, Lawrence T. *Soviet Security Interests in Europe and MFR.* April 1976. ($2.25)

73 Chubin, Shahram. *Iran's Security in the 1980s.* September 1977. ($2.25)

74 Dudzinsky, S.J., Jr. and James Digby. *New Technology and Control of Conventional Arms: Some Common Ground.* September 1977. (No charge—Reprint from *International Security*, Spring 1977)

75 Wolf, Charles, Jr. *Weapons Standardization, "Offsets," and Trade Liberalization in NATO.* September 1977. ($2.25)

76 Burt, Richard. *Nuclear Proliferation and Conventional Arms Transfers: The Missing Link.* September 1977. ($2.25)

77 Ellsworth, Robert. *New Imperatives for the Old Alliance.* December 1977. ($2.25)

78 Digby, James. *New Weapons and the Dispersal of Military Power.* September 1978. ($2.25)

Index

About the Authors

Robert F. Bacher is a Professor of Physics, Emeritus, and former Provost at California Institute of Technology. He headed the Experimental Physics Division and later the Bomb Physics Division at Los Alamos during World War II. Later he served as a Scientific Advisor to Bernard Baruch during the discussion of the U.S. proposals in the United Nations Atomic Energy Commission. He has served as a member of the first U.S. Atomic Energy Commission, 1946–1949; the President's Science Advisory Committee, 1953–1955, and 1957–1960; and numerous advisory committees and panels for the Department of Defense and the State Department. He received his Ph.D. from the University of Michigan in 1930 and has held appointments at the Massachusetts Institute of Technology, University of Michigan, Columbia University, and Cornell University. A recipient of the President's Medal for Merit in 1946, he has been a trustee of the Carnegie Corporation, the Institute for Defense Analyses, and the Rand Corporation.

Victor Gilinsky is a Commissioner on the Nuclear Regulatory Commission in Washington, D.C. He received his B.S. in Engineering Physics from Cornell University in 1956 and his Ph.D. in Theoretical Physics from California Institute of Technology in 1961, and he has conducted research on plasma physics, detection of electromagnetic and acoustic signals from nuclear explosions, civilian nuclear developments in the United States and abroad, nuclear proliferation, and technology and politics. The former head of the Physical Science Department at Rand Corporation, 1973–1974, he has also been Assistant Director for Policy Analysis and Program Review, Office

of Planning and Analysis, U.S. Atomic Energy Commission, 1972–
1973; Special Assistant to the Director of Regulations, U.S. Atomic
Energy Commission, 1971; Co-Project Leader, International Aspects
of Nuclear Energy, Rand Corporation, 1969–1971; and a Research
Fellow in Engineering, California Institute of Technology, 1970.

Robert Gillette is a science writer for the *Los Angeles Times*. He
received his Bachelor of Arts degree from the University of California
at Berkeley in 1966. Positions he has held include reporter for
Science magazine in Washington, science writer for the *San Francisco
Examiner*, and science writer for the *Toledo Blade*. Honors he has
received include an appointment as a Neiman Fellow at Harvard
University in 1975–1976, a *Los Angeles Times* Editorial Award in
1978, and the Science in Society Award from the National Associa-
tion of Science Writers in 1973. He shared the Forum Award of the
American Physical Society with the *Science* news staff in 1975.

Albert Wohlstetter is University Professor at the University of
Chicago and Co-Director of Research with Professor Henry S. Rowen
at Pan Heuristics. An author of many studies of the political, economic, and military consequences of both civilian and military
nuclear energy, he has twice been awarded the Department of Defense medal for Distinguished Public Service. He is a member of the
Executive Committee of the California Seminar on Arms Control and
Foreign Policy and has served as consultant to the State Department,
the Department of Defense, the Budget Bureau, the Arms Control
and Disarmament Agency, and the Rand Corporation, and was a
staff member of the Rand Corporation from 1953 to 1962. His
academic career includes appointments as a Fellow of All Souls
College, Oxford University; Professor in Residence at UCLA; and
Ford Professor at the University of California at Berkeley.

Roberta Wohlstetter is an author and researcher in the fields of
military history and foreign policy. Much of her past work has
focused on crises and the uses and limits of intelligence in decision-
making; her more recent work has dealt with nuclear spread. She
has been an advisor to the Assistant Secretary of Defense for International Security Affairs and has lectured at Harvard University,
Barnard College, and the University of Chicago. A member of the
New York Council on Foreign Relations, the International Institute
for Strategic Studies, the Research Council of the Georgetown
Center for Strategic and International Studies, and a vice chairman
of the Chicago Council on Foreign Relations, she graduated from

Vassar College and received graduate degrees from Columbia University and Radcliffe College. She received the Bancroft Prize in history in 1962 and the *Los Angeles Times* Woman of the Year award in 1963, and is the author of *Pearl Harbor: Warning and Decision* (Stanford University Press, 1962).